PRAISE FOR *The ...*

"His life unraveled and running helped him stitch it back together. A fascinating yarn about dealing with the devil and against all odds emerging victorious."

- **Dean Karnazes**, Acclaimed Endurance Athlete and *New York Times* Bestselling Author of **Ultramarathon Man**.

"In a world of platforms and pedestals, Malcolm isn't just a commentator when it comes to the subject of endurance, he's a living breathing embodiment. Whether you're running toward something or away from it, Malcolm's honest and gripping story will convince you to keep going."

- **CJ Casciotta**, Founder of **Sounds Like A Movement**.

The Second Lap

Going the Distance in the Race of Life

Malcolm McLoughlin

Porch Lantern Books

© 2015 Malcolm McLoughlin.

All rights reserved.

No part of this publication may be reproduced, stored in a retrieval system, or transmitted in any way by any means—electronic, mechanical, photocopy, recording, or otherwise— except for brief quotations for critical reviews or articles, without the prior permission of the copyright holder.

Some of the names in this story have been changed to protect identity. All dates and happenings are subject to memory and every effort has been made to authenticate their veracity.

First published in France by Porch Lantern Books.

This title may be purchased in bulk for educational, business, or promotional use.

Further information and purchasing can be found at

www.malcolmmcloughlin.com

twitter: @malcolmwriter

ISBN 978-2-9548070-0-3
e-book ISBN 978-2-9548070-1-0

Cover photo © Christian Harberts
Author photo © Jenn Whiteman
Design: Daron Short

To Dylan and Pearl

Contents

Acknowledgments ix

Prologue xiii

Chapter 1: Command/Control 1
Chapter 2: Helve 10
Chapter 3: Shakeout 21
Chapter 4: Shaft of Light 31
Chapter 5: Scraping the Sky 40
Chapter 6: Roots 57
Chapter 7: Against 61
Chapter 8: Life Trails 71
Chapter 9: Inroads 86
Chapter 10: Unwritten 92
Chapter 11: Relentless 102
Chapter 12: Mic Check 107
Chapter 13: Formation 118
Chapter 14: The Ledge 128

Contents

Chapter 15: Rapture 138
Chapter 16: Searching. 146
Chapter 17: Rainbows. 153
Chapter 18: "What I want for Christmas, only
    you can give me". 164
Chapter 19: Seed to Seedling. 172
Chapter 20: Replenish. 183
Chapter 21: Arc. 190
Chapter 22: Strength and Beyond 199
Chapter 23: Honour 215
Chapter 24: Letting Go 230
Chapter 25: Yield. 239
Chapter 26: When Faith Conquers Fear. 245

Epilogue 253

Acknowledgments

NO STORY IS complete without a cast of characters and I have been truly blessed in my life with the amazing people I have met and continue to meet. I thank you one and all for the paths we have crossed and the times we have shared. It is impossible to thank all of you and if I missed you, sorry! To Dylan and Pearl, wow. How could I be more blessed? Dylan, your kindness and sensitivity inspire me to be a better father. Pearl, you have taught me patience and compassion beyond measure. To my parents, John and Florrie, you have always supported me regardless of my interests and this book has been no exception. I love you both so much. My sisters and brothers, Susan and her husband Paul, Simon, Alison, and Sean (aka Jack Septiceye), you have filled my life with laughter and

The Second Lap

memories of growing up that shape the person I am today. Y'all rock.

Trev, my constant friend and unwavering supporter, I love you man, so much. Thank you for always believing in me and pushing me to reach my best. The Cpt and The W, how rare it is to have friendships that span all distance and time. Tim Meier, you came into my life and walked with me through the darkest valley of them all, it is your 'footprints' I see when I look back on my path. Alicia, sorry for all you put up with during my addiction, heartfelt thanks for all you do for our kids. Carmel, Maria, Therese, and Sinead, you have always loved me and accepted me and I am so proud of you all for surviving with dignity the things you have been through. Neil, Derek, Poochie, and Brian from TLH, Mick and Mark Kilgallon, the Fox family.

Josh and Jenn Whiteman and family, you not only fed my stomach during the writing process but also my soul. The talent and humility you both have is astounding. Tony and Raeni Roos and family. What can I say? Never was there a door more open to a stray like me. Jerry and Shelly Kragt and family for your proofing skills and the book title. Charlie Engle who got me back on the wagon after I fell hard. Thanks also to Paco and Leslie, Jim and Linda Latimer, Diana and Reid Pratt, Rachel Meier, Al and Hels, Ben and Irene, Mullenix, Schuh, Stuart, Burkes, Goepp, and Bower families. My extended family at Trinity International Church and the C&MA for

Acknowledgments

the love you have shown me. Every musician I have had the joy to play with over the years, you rocked.

Heartfelt appreciation to Patsy, Carmel, Darragh, Ian, and Karen Reams, my second family. Ciaran Guinan for giving me my first and best job and taking care of me in my teenage years. Diarmuid for all your help with Running for Pearl and advice with this book, Danny and Tanja, Daron Short, Damo and Mary Hickey, all at Brosna Press, Q and Aideen. Sally, Joe, Ian, and Gary Mahon, The Ladbroke Arms staff and patrons, Bibiche and Johann, Mamie, Nana Claudine, John Stumbo, Ben Stewart, Carson Nyquist, pastor Al and Carol, Christian Harberts, Leslie Slater, René Ghosh, CJ Casciotta, Sam Toweel Moore for being light, Stephane Rodriguez, the online friends I've never met but fill my sails with their words of encouragement. Bruce Galpin, my brother at Porch Lantern and Social-IT-e Media who maintain my website. Thank you Pearl Jam for being the soundtrack to my life.

Special thanks to my editor Clifton Wiens for his astute eyes and words of encouragement and to Michael Flood for taking a gamble on me.

To my one true love Val, you make my heart soar and every day I have to remind myself that you are mine. You are more than the woman of my dreams, you are His daughter and the perfect partner for this journey called life. You worked tirelessly on this book, I would never have made it without your encouragement. I love you.

Father, Son and Holy Spirit for leading me home.

Prologue

THE MATTRESS SPRINGS groaned under my shifting weight, while the wooden bed frame's sharp-angled edge dug into my ribs. My heavy, throbbing head swayed like an over-laden tree branch, purging and retching vomit and bile into the half-full, stinking plastic bag on the grainy wooden floor. My eyes stung with tears and sweat. The bedroom, illuminated only by sparse shafts of light poking through the shutters, felt like a dungeon, my mind felt like a prison. I was alive. Crap!

Six days earlier my wife and I had finally called time on our seven-year marriage after months of arguing and sharpshooting at each other. Soon after she flew to Dubai for work, I flew into a booze-filled marathon. It was a Saturday afternoon. Stumbling into the kitchen an hour later, I would find the entire

The Second Lap

contents of the fridge empty—thirty-two half-litre cans of beer drunk in a single day. No recollection of getting my kids to bed, let alone myself. Oh man, the kids!

I could hear my daughter Pearl in the living room. I squinted at the clock. It was midday. The kids were probably still in their pyjamas and hungry.

"Dylan," I thought I was shouting, but it came out as a feeble croak. The padding of slippered feet approached the door and as my son rounded the corner, his fearful eyes tore through me. How must I look to my six-year-old? Unable to put a sentence together, I started to dry heave again; Dylan burst into tears. I tried to hold my hand up to signal it was OK, that it would pass, and that I would get better. But how many times had he seen this? How many occasions had he wondered why I was so frequently ill in this way? The answer was too many. I could not tear myself away from alcohol. God knows I had tried hard over the past fourteen years.

The phone rang in the other room. It probably was the kids' mother calling from Dubai.

Oh, no! I thought to myself, *She must be checking in to say hi to Dylan and Pearl.* In spite of my inner dialogue, I was still so drunk that I couldn't make a move towards answering the phone so that they could talk to their mom. I couldn't even tell Dylan to answer for me. He just stood frozen in fear. I had finally, after half-a-life of addiction, come face to face with the fabled 'rock bottom' that addicts in my AA meetings had talked about as if it was some sort of

Prologue

twisted epiphany. Their gin-binging stories ranging from lost jobs to manslaughter made me want to get even more drunk. At times I was tempted to invite them out for a beer afterwards. AA did not make me want to drink less, *au contraire*. I left each meeting dreaming about an IV infusion of Tanqueray, squeezing the bag like an empty tube of toothpaste in order to get every single drop. AA hadn't worked, so what hope did I have now? My son continued his forlorn stare at me.

"Papa please stop drinking, I don't want you to die."

Dylan's words dropped like an anvil on my dazed mind. My son's plea that day impacted me more than the birth of my two children or my wedding vows. The naked truth of my child hurting, and I was the one hurting him, ripped at my heart. How though could I salve his wounds and mine? How could I rebuild my self-esteem after the myriad of lies my life had become? I barely knew who *I* was any more. An internal voice, a soft velvet whisper, cut through the blur. *This is your last chance.* I believed it more than I can explain to this day. I would have to learn how to live again, to make myself from the ground up. I would have to walk the long road but, I had decided, the most important part was choosing to survive. It would take all the willpower and strength that I was not even sure I had. I took my son's little hand in mine, and made the most important and infinitesimal motion of my life, the first step.

1

Command/Control

THE FIRST TIME I geared myself up to drop acid, I was cautious. And with good reason. Horror stories of people going out of their mind with paranoia and imagining themselves covered in rats or snakes were just a few of many nightmare scenarios I'd heard about acid trips. LSD wasn't like alcohol or smoking a joint where if you got too messed up, you could rein it in by stopping or puking. Acid was all or nothing. Once the dose was taken there was no turning back. If it went pear-shaped, then there was no choice but to hold on and ride it out. While there was plenty of it available in Athlone when I decided this would be my next drug of choice, I didn't feel like the mood there would be conducive for my début trip.

The Second Lap

Dublin would be the place. I had gotten to know some folks through the music scene in Tullamore who were going to college there. We had started mountain biking together at Charleville Castle. One night, on an impromptu camping trip after an afternoon on our bikes, we were talking over beers and joints around the campfire. The subject turned to magic mushrooms and acid. One guy, Gric, had a heap of stories from his own experiences. The depth and vividness of his narrative had us enthralled. If taking it to the next level was my objective, he said this was the way to do it. So on that night, it was decided that a few weeks later I'd take the train to Dublin where about fifteen of us would take the helter-skelter down the yellow brick road together. I said nothing to the guys in the band or any of my friends because I knew I'd probably get a lecture on the dangers of dipping my toes into uncharted waters. My mind couldn't have been changed anyway. If it turned out to be a disaster, then I'd have only myself to blame. When the appointed weekend came, I finished up on the Friday evening and grabbed a beer with a girl who was in my publishing class. I really liked Rose. She was different than any other girl I'd met. I had a girlfriend and was completely faithful, but I was seventeen years old and was not about to get married. I just loved going for drinks with this mysterious girl in my course. She had a certain maturity and was in her way like me, an outsider. I think she felt something was there too, but she had a boyfriend and a big one at that.

Command/Control

He was older than her, and she let me know straight up that if he knew we were getting cosy in a bar, he would snap my neck like a twig. I didn't need my head twisted off by some muscle man; I needed my head opened in a psychedelic way. So I left her at the bar and headed toward my new drug of choice for the weekend.

Arriving in Dublin that night to hook up with my new friends blew doors in my mind that hitherto had been closed and cobwebbed. The pure sharing of love and respect between us put me in a wonderful frame of mind to go on this adventure. I was introduced all around to easy going, smiling guys and gals with strange names and colourful clothes. You could spot me straight away through the cloud of dope smoke as the new guy. I was the only one who looked like he'd brushed his hair or had a shower that day, or in some of their cases, that month. Joints were passed. Cider and beer swigged from large bottles. It was one of those moments when no one cares about the past or the future, it was that moment alone that mattered.

I usually was fretting over drum payments, or missing a bus, or whether everything in the future would work out for me. Not with this group, and it was through spending time with them, I realised that I occasionally could just let go. I took off my wristwatch and placed it in a drawer for the weekend. I was going on my mission without time restraint.

At about eight thirty that evening, it was declared time to drop our acid. My new friend Tom explained

The Second Lap

that it was tiny squares of paper dipped in LSD and usually called tabs. He took a small colourful square of paper from his pocket and showed me the evening menu. 'Strawberries' were the lightest on offer and were named so because of the image of a strawberry on the front. His reckoning was that this would be the best place for me to start as I was an acid virgin. I didn't argue with him and agreed with his choice. When I asked him what he was planning, he produced another square of paper called 'Aliens' which sure enough had a little black alien on the front similar to the ones I'd seen on an Atari video game when I was younger. These tabs were supposed to have a kick that I wasn't ready to feel just yet. Already high from the hash and the booze, the twelve of us dropped our tabs and took off from the apartment in one big line like a trail of ants heading to work. It was such a communal experience and I knew I was in the best possible hands to take my sensory perception to the limit.

We were walking up the hill towards Dublin's largest green space, the Phoenix Park, when I felt a kick. Actually, it was more of a nudge, a teasing glimmer of what was to come. My mouth had suddenly become dry and I just could not keep the smile from my face. When I laid my hand on my fellow tripper Fern's shoulder, she turned around with a smile to match. "Holy shit!!!" I exclaimed to her, which she countered with a giggling fit and started screaming to the guys walking ahead that "Mally has just come up." A lot of attention was

Command/Control

sent my way with hugs and talk of my being one of them now and that our night would be unparalleled in the history of the universe. And this was only the beginning. Once we arrived at the park, the sun was going down on this perfect summer evening. The sea of open green space reached out to caress my body like a womb. I was about two hours in now, and my mental stimulation was heightened more than at any other time in my life. As they ran and played in the grass like kids, I could feel a wave of joy wash over me every time they touched the long grass. The sound of voices came in the form of colours, and laughter brought tears of joy. This was euphoria. I spoke to no one in particular stating, "I should be doing this all the time."

The reason the world was so cruel and messed up was because more people didn't go tripping. I spouted complex theories to a rapt audience and conjured the purest truths from my mind, my tongue delivering my genius in streams of eloquent prose. I wanted to live in this state for the rest of my life. What was I doing attending computer courses and wasting my time in a room with a bunch of others who couldn't see they were being screwed every day by the *system*? I felt a connectedness to the earth on an oceanic scale with all the boundaries of my other life washed away. Hours passed that could have been minutes and minutes that could have been hours. I celebrated this invincibility by telling Tom I was ready to take another. This time I took an 'Alien.' In a world of rationality it was the worst thing I

The Second Lap

could have done, but my logic had been left back home. I continued to sway and feel psychologically amplified until the second dose came knocking at the door. When it hit, I could barely keep it together and my eyes were dilated to huge dark saucers. I became quiet and a little more withdrawn. My earlier garrulousness was replaced with hyper-vigilance and I watched every twitch and move my friends made. The more I sat there, the more anxious and sensitised I became. We had moved over to a large dome-shaped seating area that had a roof hanging over a long bench. I sat on the floor and the more my friends talked, the more I watched the reflection of the moonlight on their faces. Facial expressions started to change and become wolf-like as I repeated the same mantra over and over again: *It's just the drugs Mally, hold on.* When the sun came up we were coming down and faced with the long walk back to the city centre. That walk was pure torture. Drugs are just like the laws of gravity, what goes up has gotta come back down.

The first part of me to feel it, outside of the mental anguish, was my stomach. I felt nauseous and my insides churned like someone had tied a knot in there. The thought of food was appealing but the physical act of eating was not yet possible. On arrival at the apartment, one of the girls laid me down on the sofa and went for orange juice at a shop. I couldn't fathom how anyone in the state we were in could go talk to someone behind a counter. Obviously she had done it before so it

Command/Control

was probably no big deal for her. She returned with the orange juice and some vitamin C pills for me. After sipping a couple glasses of juice, I felt slightly better. Joints were rolled to take the edge off and we sat smoking with some ambient music to penetrate the silence. My acid high was stratospheric, but the low pummelled me. I felt very depressed in the days that followed after my return to reality and rarely spoke unless spoken to. I took acid intermittently over the next two or three years but never sought it out. If the mood was right at a party and I had no courses or work for a while, I would accept a light tab and go with the flow. I also watched people who continued with regular doses and upped it until it became a sort of reality for them. However, it all ended badly. Friends from that group started to withdraw completely. No mind can take that prolonged out-of-control-thinking.

As my time at the training centre came to an end, we were obliged to go out and find work experience one day per week. I chose a printing company in Ferbane called The Brosna Press where I developed friendships and respect for people that changed my attitudes towards many things. The Guinan family had been in the printing business for 35 years. When the father, Kieran, passed away, his sons Diarmuid and Ciaran took the reins. Ciaran, or Brownie as he was known, was a local legend who sang beautifully and fronted a Cajun Country band which packed pubs and halls wherever they went. Diarmuid was the creative brains behind the press. A more gifted

The Second Lap

graphic designer I've yet to meet. He was a mean jazz singer to boot. In fact, the whole family was blessed with great voices and the ability to make an instrument soar. I had no idea who they were when I sloped in the door one day asking for a few hours a week. Brownie was as amiable a person I could have hoped for as an employer and he agreed to give me a chance on the spot.

I was still hammering out music with the boys and we were getting places with gigs by playing lots of different towns. With my course coming to an end, I said an emotional goodbye to my friends and readied myself for a full-time job in the printing business. I was made to feel very welcome and the humour there suited me. In addition, the work was really interesting. A local named Damo was to be my mentor, and he was hilarious, full to the brim with stories of drinking and meeting girls. When it came to his work, though, he was meticulous and taught me how not to settle for average. The thing that kept that business alive and what continues to make it thrive to this day is the care and passion that goes into every detail. Being surrounded by that tends to rub off and I wanted to be a part of what made them great. I learned quickly and was soon taking on greater responsibility with important book contracts. Yes, I printed raffle tickets too, but this was where I wanted to be in my life. I was making more money than ever before and was able to pay off Charlie at the music store a lot quicker.

Command/Control

It was a great time to be a musician, too. The Irish economy was going strong and the pubs were packed out from Thursday through Sunday. People liked their beer and their music and so did we. My gig routine consisted of having a joint, setting up the kit, and downing a few pints of Heineken. The beer and dope gave me the edge to push the limits of my performance. Trev was my partner in all things, and we matched each other drink for drink and smoke for smoke. The chemistry between all of us as a unit was bordering on telepathic. The size of the audience made no difference, if it was five or two hundred and five, we scorched places like no one before. The extra cash that we made went back to the bar for more beers. Trev and I were the ones who partied most. The better the gig, the more shots and pints we slammed back. I'd wake up on some floor with a mouth as dry as the carpet to which my tongue was stuck. My horizons seemed limitless, and the fish-bowl life of the small town was beginning to weigh. Eventually I'd seek adventure elsewhere, I just wasn't sure where.

2

Helve

TREV WAS ROCKING from side to side. He kept placing his hands over his ears and had trouble standing. I put him in a sitting position with his head between his legs and wondered if he was going to bounce back. I'd seen him shaken up before but not like this. He needed to get it together, and fast. We were in Schilpol Airport, Amsterdam—the great city of legal drugs, trams, citizenry on bikes, and hookers in the Red-Light District windows. The irony was not lost on me that Trev was in this condition, and we had just *arrived*. It was August 1997 and he and I were twenty-one and twenty-years-old respectively. Hedonism beckoned. After a couple of years of playing gigs, we had decided that it was time we went on a journey together. I picked the destination, grabbed some

Helve

money from him and booked the tickets. Trev was happy that we were going to spend a whole week getting stoned, as was I. Less exciting for him was the prospect of getting into a metal tube with wings. He hated heights, and he knew he was in for a world of pain as soon as we took off. He had psyched himself out so much beforehand that it took a few Heineken at the airport to convince him he could get through it. Armed with a slab of chewing gum and plenty of liquids for popping ears, we boarded. What followed bordered on comical. A best friend in pain is my pain too, but because I had been flying regularly from a young age, I found it hard not to chuckle.

The main reason I had chosen Amsterdam was not based on decadence, but because my dear friend Danny had moved there a few years earlier to live with his girlfriend, Tanja. Danny is an incredibly dedicated musician and he is also the brother of Brownie and Diarmuid. While others were farting around playing dead-end pubs, he was making albums and going on tour. And his stuff was good. It wasn't a case of "he's my friend, so I have to like his material." When he put his heart into a gig, you could hear a pin drop in the place. I had been really sad when he left Ireland but knew he needed to give the European circuit a go. Who could blame him? Part of me wanted to get out myself, but I also reasoned I was young and time was on my side.

Trev and I were headed to meet up with Danny. There was just the small matter of the flight to get through first. Take off was murder: Trev looked

The Second Lap

like a guy you avoid at all costs, a deranged lunatic being extradited back to the land of tulips. Once the plane levelled out and he got some semblance of inner ear comfort back, he seemed to stabilise. Then the pilot took a severe right turn and banked hard. Trev cursed the guy to hell and back. He even remembered that flight and that pilot for years to come. He swore that if he ever flew again and the voice on the intercom before take-off was that pilot's, he would get off the plane.

Landing proved to be the undoing of his already fragile head. His ears were pounding and his sense of balance was out of sync. I'd managed to get our bags and get us through customs, assuring him he would be fine later. And there he sat, with his back to the window of a sports shop as travellers passed by (he cursed them too) with big smiles and beer in their eyes. I told Trev to man up, we had work to do. We took a stroll to get some air and hopped on the train to Dam Square. The hostel proved easy enough to locate once we worked out which direction to take the tram.

Dutch. People. Rock. Those three words are enough to make a person go back time after time. They speak killer English, have a great sense of humour, and are really friendly. Before we arrived, I didn't know what to expect. Amsterdam was mainland Europe. I had been to England numerous times and a holiday resort in Spain (which was like being in England, only with sunburned partiers drinking all night and sleeping all day). That didn't

Helve

qualify as embracing a different culture. I wanted art, canals, history, weed, and beer. No small order.

Our hostel was clean and cheap and close to everything we needed to see. The first person we met was a fellow-traveller named Chad. He was tall and super good-looking with long hair and told us he came from California. He asked us what our plans were for the evening to which we replied it would be a chilled evening with a few beers to recover from the flight. He was having none of it and took it upon himself to be our tour guide. He escorted us to the Red-Light District. We were both baffled and in awe.

There before us—shop after shop—and separated only by a pane of glass stood gyrating women of every race, shape, and age. They teased and waved and beckoned for business, and business looked good. Here was the oldest profession in the world being performed in a clean, safe, and efficient way. Say what you want about prostitution, but in my mind it was better than some scumbag treating a girl like dirt in a grimy alley. They had the control and there was less risk than walking the street corners.

Our little tour finished and we headed to what would be our main haunt for the week, 'The Bulldog.' It was located on the left hand side of a canal from the direction we came and when we stepped into the haze, the place was booming. Music vibrations reverberated throughout the wooden interior. Behind the counter stood a tag-team of two of the most laid-back guys we had ever met. Chad was advising us on the different types of weed and the

The Second Lap

effects they had. The Bulldog had a menu which I just could not get over. How many times had I stood on a street corner back home waiting for a friend to drop me off some hash in the middle of the night? Too many. This was primo weed and it was on a *freaking menu* for crying out loud! I have no recollection of what we chose but I do know that we were cocky and considered ourselves dedicated smokers. To top it off, we selected two of the biggest beers in the house. When the guy with the ponytail and crooked teeth put two *buckets* of the local brew in front of us, we just stuck out our chests and manly strolled over to a high table where Chad had sat down. We had made it; it was time to see how the folks of the 'dam' rolled.

We sipped our large beers and hand-rolled some joints whilst chatting animatedly about our lives back home. Chad talked about women, parties, drugs, women, parties, and maybe drugs again. It was nice to have broken the ice because once we lit those joints all talking vanished into the air like the plumes of smoke we were exhaling. This was the greenest and smoothest weed known to man, or to us at least. It was as if some Rasta had cultivated it on his own personal farm and pruned off only the most select buds for me and my pal. It was very close to the acid experience in terms of its newness and deepened introspection. It took just one joint and one beer to absolutely destroy us. Eventually Chad took off to score some girls. Trev and I, we just stared at the walls in silence.

Helve

Then, I needed to go to the toilet. I nodded at Trev and left him at the table. After finishing my business, I turned to walk out. I pushed the door, and it wouldn't budge. Not a good omen considering how completely off my head I was. I tried jigging the lock and pushing on the handle but still nothing. I pushed harder and harder and contemplated kicking the door down to escape. I was starting to sweat. The beats of the music had the walls of the bathroom pulsating, what was I to do? I was abandoning all hope of getting out and had been inside for over fifteen minutes. Then I heard a light tap on the door before it pushed *in* on me. Another customer was waiting to use it. I had spent a quarter of an hour pushing the door when a simple pull would have sufficed. That's stoned. In Amsterdam. Like I said, it was good stuff.

Surviving our first night there, we quickly established a routine. We would wake and shower, then make small talk with the other people in our room and go for a milkshake at McDonald's. The milkshakes were a lifesaver. The coldness and cream settled our stomachs from all the booze. After that we would stroll to our favourite eatery where they made the most killer omelettes. We consumed so many eggs at that eatery that if the alcohol or drugs didn't kill us, our cholesterol levels eventually would. After that we would take our full stomachs on a tour of the city, stopping regularly for beers and, of course, a few smokes. Our tolerances for various potencies improved rapidly. We chose a different weed menu

The Second Lap

each day. Days two and three we ended up in The Bulldog as now they knew us there. It was like the TV show *Cheers*, but on drugs, and *nobody* knew your name.

By the end of the fourth day though, it was clear we needed to change things up a bit. We had started the morning by meeting Neil, a Texan, who was a friend of Chad's. Chad was leaving to continue his European tour and rack up a few more notches on his hostel bedpost. Hence, he shunted Neil onto us. Neil was one of those guys who follows you around like a puppy. He was a real nice guy, but we were looking for action. Neil put a damper on that. Then, roaming the streets we bumped into a friend of Neil's from his hostel. Her name was Maria, and she was from "Thili."

"Sorry, where did you say you were from?"
"Thili."
"Never heard of it, girl."
"Sure you have, everyone knows Thili."
"Listen, I might be stoned, but I have *never* heard of THILI!"

Neil had to intervene, and he explained it a little clearer to us. "Ah, you're from *Chile*, why didn't you just say so?" Being high and Spanish accents are evidently not a good combination. Maria was on a mission to take some magic mushrooms, and a light bulb went on over everyone's head. Why hadn't we thought of this beforehand? There was even a shop across the street from our hostel called 'Dr. Paddo's Magic Mushroom Shop' and, not to be outdone by

Helve

the weed sellers, he too had a menu proffering the finest fungi in Amsterdam. Various bags were bought and we hit the park to get it on. The sun was splitting the rocks that day, and it had been an exceptionally hot week in the capital. The park was a beautiful area with winding paths, roller-blading beauties, trees for shade, and plenty of space to space out in. We bought a few cans of soda to wash down the mushrooms and settled into conversation for the arrival of an afternoon in technicolour. It was the first time Trev and I had done mushrooms. From the way Maria had been talking earlier, she was not new to this. Only it turns out, she was. As soon as we had swallowed down our 'shrooms, stalks and all, she started to get anxious. She was pacing a little bit and talking really fast. There was nothing anyone could say to bring her back to the ground and she was soon ranting aggressively at us. The last thing I remember seeing was Trev swatting away the planes that were flying around his head; Neil was having a conversation with his backpack; I was up to my knees in the lake chasing ducks and Maria, dear, dear Maria was running against the flow of various skaters, cyclists, and runners, parting them like Moses and the Red Sea, with her arms flailing and screaming at the top of her voice that "they" were coming to get her. Turns out there were no pond, ducks, or planes, and that Neil's bag didn't have any magical gift of speech. To be more stringent with the truth, he didn't actually *have* a backpack with him. As for Maria from *Thili*, well, we didn't see her again.

The Second Lap

I felt bad the morning after, and my hangover doled out the punishment. To finish ourselves off in style, we had found a seedy bar to give the remnants of the drugs a good soaking. We had left as the sun came up, Trev and I stumbling the streets of Amsterdam carrying each other. The city was starting to hammer us and we needed a break, badly.

Danny and Tanja came to the rescue at exactly the right time; we had been on a non-stop rampage through the city for four days, and we needed to pull back. Danny gave us instructions on how to get to Haarlem from Amsterdam. Were we glad to see him when we got off the train. He took us to a nice pub called 'The Studio' where he gigged regularly and all the locals knew him. After catching up on old times and polishing off a healthy few pints of Dutch Guinness, it was back to Danny's for supper. Tanja was happy to see us. They were expecting their first child in a matter of weeks so she was carrying a big belly. Some other friends of theirs stopped by for drinks and the change of pace and intimacy of the night surpassed the mindless tomfoolery of the past few days. Danny's Dutch was very good and I was impressed by how he had moved to a different country and fit in so well. His transition to the Netherlands would inspire me continually in the years that followed. The next day was a scorcher. Tanja wanted to take us to the beach which was only a short drive away. We crammed into their car, the windows down, and the 'Presidents of the USA' blaring on the stereo. You know those experiences

Helve

in life that are so filled with joy and wonder that you feel like you're in a movie, except it's real and tangible? Where the air is alive with laughter and there is a vibe of appreciation for being in the perfect place at the perfect time? It was that sort of a day; it went deep for me. Certain connections defy explication; I'm unable to capture a mood like that in words.

The beach was busy. Trev and I found a bar called 'Woodstock' at the end of a row of beach-front shops and cafés, while Danny and Tanja stayed on the beach to catch the rays. Woodstock lived up to its name: topless people strolled around passing joints to each other or played some of the many bongos that littered the room. It was a plain and open space for sandy-toed people to come in and get high. Needless to say we were not impolite and joined in with gusto.

We spent one more night with our dear friends before going back to Amsterdam for our last night. It was not a full-on frenzy this time. The days with our friends slowed us down to a less breakneck pace. We were happy just to return to The Bulldog, say good-bye to those guys, and have a few smokes and a beer or six. As a parting gift, they were kind enough to give us one of the pre-rolled joints they specialised in. It was nuclear. As soon as we lit it up, there was a body count of two. We were so wasted after a few puffs that I don't think we even finished it. We had taken on Amsterdam, and we had been trounced. But in another way it was a total victory:

The Second Lap

we had spent every waking minute together with not even so much as a disagreement. I couldn't ascertain if my lungs were sore from the week of smoking or from the week of laughter. When Trev hopped on that plane for the return, he was worried, but he survived the flight like a champion. Older friendships had been reignited and new ones made. Minds had been opened and humbled, and above all we made it back safely into the lives we lived in Ireland. Could things get any better?

3

Shakeout

SOMETIMES LIFE HITS an apex and then plateaus for a while. Sometimes life can seem like a mountain ascent. Sections may be tough, but it keeps going upward. The next four years felt like I was climbing ever closer to the summit of Mt. Everest.

I was playing the drums with precision and power and we had started to play big biker festivals with a reputation as a band which crushed it every single time. I had turned twenty-one years old and had an epic party with the closest people in the world to me. My sister Susan had gotten married and I was the best man, a truly special day for our family. Life was good and my workmate Damo had returned from a year long sabbatical in Australia, telling me of the bounties that awaited those clever enough

The Second Lap

to apply for a visa and go seek them out. The dope smoking ebbed and flowed and was not something I needed all the time, but I always had that relationship with drugs, whether it was acid, weed, ecstasy, or mushrooms. I could do them for a while to see how it affected my philosophical approach to life, but it wasn't a hardcore addiction. What I loved was to drink beer. I *loved* it, the taste, how it made me feel, the social aspect of it, the ritual of it all.... Drinking was my thing. I wasn't an addict, hell no; I just liked to drink all night and occasionally get up on the weekends and have a beer first thing in the morning to jump start my body and stave off the eventual hangover for just another hour or so, at least until I had a shower. That's not too much to ask for, right?

Trev and I made a second trip to Amsterdam a year after our first and it was a disaster. We stayed in a hostel where people were shooting up heroin in the corner of the room. We got mugged. It was messy. Serena, my steady girlfriend of four years, and I had broken up and I needed a new challenge to keep the momentum in my life going. I was afraid if I stood still for long enough that boredom would catch up with me and quench this flame I had burning inside. On a random Saturday night out with Damo and his friends, I saw my brother Simon's English teacher who I thought was really hot. Her name was Laura and she was older than me by a few years. She looked bored at the club and so was I. We got to talking about books and really hit it off. The first kiss turned

Shakeout

into a few months of really good times but when she took off for Australia, I was pretty beaten up about it. I felt we had really connected and now life felt emptier. Long letters were exchanged and the loneliness of her outback wanderings seemed to be getting to her too. I decided the only thing to do was get a visa and follow her. I went through the very complicated procedure of applying and got my visa after a six-week wait. The next thing to do was tell my boss. Brownie's heart sank. Here was another one of his printers leaving the country to chase girls and get drunk every night. However, he didn't try to stop me. He wished me the best—the greatest boss ever, that man. I booked my tickets to Darwin, Australia, for mid-October and still had a few months to wait before I could go and see my girl. During this period of time I worked hard and saved hard, rarely going out for big drinking sessions with the guys. I'd get my beers cheap and sit in front of the TV with my dad, who was the best person to chill with. I spoke to Laura a few times on the phone. Then one call seemed strange. I replayed the conversation over and over and read between the lines of all her letters. I told myself I was just nervous and to keep calm. A few days later, the letter came. She was sorry, but she simply wanted to be friends. When I spoke to her the next day on the phone she explained. She had met Mark and was very enamoured by him.

"Enamoured!" All I could picture was my foot on his windpipe. I went for a walk that night and contemplated doing something stupid. Instead of

The Second Lap

something stupid, I grabbed a few beers and sat down in my room with my journal, I poured it all out on a page and fell asleep in my clothes at four A.M.

The plan of action? Go to Australia and live it up to the maximum. My best buddies threw me a going away party that lasted two days. The girls responsible, Maria, Therese, Sinead, and Carmel came into my life a few years earlier on a bus home from a rock night. They wore T-shirts of my favourite bands, combat boots, and looked cool compared to all the other chicks with their layered make-up and miniskirts. We bonded over music, alcohol, and a passion for the good things in life. Busking around camp fires and listening to Jeff Buckley and Leonard Cohen together was the norm. They were and still are like sisters to me. My party was an enormous gathering at our local drinking spot, The Vine House, in Banagher. We filled it to capacity and sang songs with the band that played for us. My heart felt heavy with emotion leaving them behind. Our beautiful friend Patrick had tragically drowned a few weeks before and we were not only raw with grief still, but also worried for his girlfriend Denise, who had become eerily silent and reclusive. After leaving the pub, we partied into the night at Therese's place whose parents happened to be away. When the phone rang, we ignored it, assuming it was her parents calling. We partied well into the morning. I spent the next two days cramming in as many drinking sessions as I could in order to say goodbye to everyone. I had forty-eight hours to pack

Shakeout

and get myself in order before my sister, Susan, and her husband, Paul, would take me to the airport. At every pub I passed, someone appeared with a pint for me, every house I visited, a can of beer was pressed into my palm. By the time Monday morning came to leave, I was *poisoned*. I'd felt bad before from hangovers, but this one was magnified by the stress of two solid days of travel and being greeted at the other end by my ex and her new boyfriend. Susan and Paul winced the whole way on the hour and half journey to Dublin as I lay on the back seat retching into a plastic bag. I couldn't even drink water without spewing up like a geyser. How was I supposed to get on a plane in that state? Dublin to London was fine; there I changed over to fly to Hong Kong. After four hours in Hong Kong, I jumped on a flight to take me to Cairns where I would then change for Darwin. What I didn't realise was that in order to get to Cairns we had first to fly all the way down to Brisbane, refuel, take on more passengers, and then fly to Cairns. I was furious. Flying from city to city in other countries may be OK, but Australia is a desolate beast of a land, factor into the equation that I'm like a microwaved corpse and fading fast. I eventually made it to Cairns for the last flight after having my time zones put through a blender. I didn't even know what day it was. The punishing humidity of the tropics made carrying a bag for a short distance across the tarmac laborious. I checked in my things and boarded the last flight of my odyssey. By the time I arrived in Darwin it was forty-eight hours since I'd

The Second Lap

departed Dublin, thirty-six of those hours had been spent in the air. As soon as I got off the plane I was trying to figure out why the inside of the terminal building was so warm. It turned out that I wasn't inside. It was a wave of heat that I'd last felt when I opened an oven to check on a pizza.

Laura, my now-ex, was there to meet me, and strangely it felt great to see her. She took me back to the apartment that we would share with her friend Aileen. I was tired and lost but glad to be sitting down in a chair that wasn't travelling at a few hundred miles per hour over the sea. Mark came by and introductions were made. From the minute I met him, I just knew he was an awesome person. Smiling, happy, polite, and carrying his spare skateboard for me; we hit it off straight away. Laura had told him I liked to skate, and he went out of his way to make me feel welcome. It couldn't have been easy for him either. Here was his girlfriend sharing an apartment with her ex-boyfriend. When two people are right for each other, no man or woman should come between them. I saw something that she and I didn't have and it's a joy everyone in life deserves to feel.

Australia is a truly magical and original land—its grandeur in stark contrast to its small population: under twenty-two million people in over seven and a half-million square km makes for big back yards. Darwin was hot and sticky and filled with all sorts of refugees and original characters.

Laura and Aileen had decided to live there after meeting an Irish guy called Martin who helped them

Shakeout

get settled. His nice big house with a swimming pool was just down the street from us. After my first week of sleeping all day and being up all night with jet-lag, I finally met him. He was a diminutive, grey-bearded man with a Dublin accent that belied his thirty plus years in the tropics. He liked drinking beer and his son liked smoking weed. He had a bunch of hot girls from Dublin staying with him on vacation for a few days, a good distraction for my broken heart. So far, off to a good start, but once I got to know the area, I realised that there wasn't much going on. Mark would have barbecues at his place and songs, laughter, and partial nudity usually ensued. I skated a lot, but doing anything in the humidity was borderline impossible. I'd wake in the morning and walk to the local mall, then come back and take a shower, then skate a bit and need another shower. By evening time I would be sweating from doing nothing, so I'd take my third shower of the day and hit an air conditioned pub. There was never a breeze, just a weight that hung in the air. If the Aboriginal people were about, you could get their unwashed odour from about fifty metres. Most of them drank hard and I got into many an argument with the locals who hated them for being alcoholics. My philosophy was simple: they didn't fly the booze in here in the first place—it was the white man! They also stole clothes in the middle of the night from drying lines outside people's apartments. I laughed this off until one day I was coming back from the supermarket on the bus and here's this Aboriginal dude waiting to get

The Second Lap

on wearing a Pearl Jam T-shirt I'd been looking for high and low for days. I shouted after him through the window, but he fled into the bushes. I loved that T-shirt but at least he was representing Seattle's finest amongst his own tribe.

After four weeks, we were getting ready to pack and make our long journey to Melbourne. Sitting at home in the air conditioning one Sunday night, the phone rang. Laura answered it, and her tone changed in an instant. She was being reassuring and guarded to whomever she was talking to, then she handed the phone to me. It was my mother, she told me she had some news about Denise. My first question in an almost matter-of-fact way was, "Is she dead?" The answer was yes; the rest is a blur.

I met Denise as a teenager through the same friends from Banagher who got me messed up before my grand trip. Most of them studied in Galway and they had befriended Denise there instantly. She was tuned in to all the great bands, artists, writers, and comedians. She was way ahead of everyone's tastes and an absolute visionary when it boiled down to bands and off-the-wall artists. She was light years in front of all of us, and we loved her for it. She introduced me to my greatest inspiration, the late and unequalled comedian Bill Hicks, through videos and concerts he had recorded before his early death from cancer. Through clouds of smoke, we sat and listened and learned. Being with her was a masterclass in respecting yourself and your own tastes and views. I spent so many weekends at their house just

Shakeout

loving the time we shared together. When Patrick died, everything changed. Maria, Therese, and I had not seen each other for months over the summer as we had been off travelling or working. We met at The Vine House to catch-up and had just sipped our first brews when Therese's dad walked through the door with a grave expression on his face. He told us Patrick was dead, drowned; he didn't know more than that. He offered to take us to Galway immediately. The journey took an hour; it seemed like eternity. We arrived to find Denise and the rest of the crew devastated. They had been swimming in the river when a speed boat passed, sending a wave crashing down on Patrick. He was weak, having spent some time in the hospital the week before, and he went under instantly. Denise, a strong swimmer, desperately dived for him to no avail. Later that evening a dive team found him. He was in his early twenties and he was gone. The funeral and following months crushed us all. I was preparing for Australia and held on to the memories of the great times we shared. Denise never accepted it. Patrick's death had broken her soul. She took her own life at the same place she had lost her lover. She laid out her clothes for her own funeral, left a note for her close circle of friends, and even prepared the songs she wanted played on the day. A clock was stopped and left on a rock at the time she waded into the river. Her backpack was beside it. When they found her, she had her arms crossed over her chest and a serene smile on her face. The pain our friends and

The Second Lap

her family went through in the aftermath is difficult to contemplate. What I do know is that there was a debate as to whether I should be told, being several thousand miles away in Australia. In the end, my friends and my mother came to the decision that I deserved to be informed.

I think I knew Denise would never stay with us. Even so, I felt a loss beyond understanding, but she was at peace now. I phoned Sinead later that evening. Amid our tears, I could barely breathe when she explained that on that last night in Ireland at my going-away party when the phone rang, it was Denise calling to say good-bye. I never got to say *au revoir*. She was a friend who left an indelible footprint on my life and I hope to see her again someday. I promised myself that night that my trip was going to honour her and I would rip it up every single chance I got.

4

Shaft of Light

L AURA, AILEEN, AND I set off in our five-berth deluxe camper vehicle with dust and desert ahead of us. Laura had found the van as part of a relocation deal; we didn't have to pay a rental fee, only fuel costs. As long as we got the van to Sydney in one piece then everyone was happy. The plan was to drive down through the outback to Port Augusta and then swing over to Sydney, drop the camper-van there and get a train to Mark's hometown of Melbourne. We took our time and would stop in outback towns depending on how far we had travelled and how tired we felt. We had one shot at this, and I'd seen enough of the country from the air. I craved the inhospitable land and its profound barrenness. We were all on the same wavelength which made the journey a lot more

The Second Lap

relaxing. No schedule, just drive. After four and a half thousand km and enough anecdotes to fill the rest of this book, we arrived in Sydney. Although if I was to share only one story, it would be this: Coober Pedy is a town in the state of South Australia about eight hundred fifty km north of Adelaide. It is known as the opal capital of the world due to the amount of mining and mineral production that happens there. It has a very unique feature: the majority of housing is below ground because of the intense heat during the daytime. They play golf at night with luminous balls, that's how hot it gets. The locals are rough looking characters. Aboriginals loiter outside the corner shop pouring out the contents of Coke cans and refilling them with beer. When I say it looks like something out of *Mad Max: Beyond Thunderdome* I'm not exaggerating. That movie and many other sci-fi features have been filmed there because of its bleak landscape and arid conditions. We had been told upon leaving Darwin that with two women in the van, it was best to drive through Coober Pedy waving and smiling. Our van had other ideas. It had run like a clock until we were smack bang in the centre of the town when the lights promptly died and an irritating, high-pitched alarm went off in the dashboard. As we pulled into this semi-front-yard-type-space, a heap of people had gathered around to see what the drama was about. It was like a ZZ Top convention with the amount of beards on display. Women were few and far between. I don't know if we looked worried, but we were. Laura explained to

Shaft of Light

some kid what had happened and he went to get his 'old man' who turned out to be the local electrician. He had never seen a razor in his life. He popped the hood and fiddled around with a few wires while we looked on with our butts planted firmly against the van. He then asked Aileen to hop in, and when he gave the signal, she was to turn on the ignition. Now, maybe it was Aileen's nerves that got the better of her trigger finger because without even an utterance from him she turned on the ignition. There was a blast of electricity that sent him flying back as the most expletive ridden outburst I'd ever heard filled the air along with the smoke coming from his fingertips. He hopped like a Tasmanian devil for a good five minutes, and I thought, *that's it, we are going to be buried in the desert*. He shook his head and said nothing, freezing us in a breathless moment like skateboarders hanging in midair, before crashing back to reality.

He muttered something about "bloody Sheila's" but deep down it was probably the highlight of his week. It would make a great story over a few 'tinnies' at the local beer shack. We should have stayed the night given it was dusk by the time he slammed the bonnet shut, but we drove out quick-smart and never looked back. The time I spent on the road in the outback was a taste of the real Australia. I could never understand some of the Irish folks who went there for a year and worked in Sydney for eleven months, drank in the same Irish pub every day after work and went on a four-week holiday up the east

The Second Lap

coast before flying home. Every day doing the same thing is a waste of the gift of life. Challenge yourself, because someday it'll all be over.

Dropping off our van in Sydney, we took the train to Melbourne and found a great four-bedroom house on a quaint little road called Baker Street. It was airy, had a lemon tree and a barbecue out the back and the neighbours were cool. I found a job at a local printing company. I didn't know it at the time, but printing was the most sought-after profession in the area. On my first interview, I was hired on the spot by a guy called Mark F. He was a mullet-sporting, motorbike-riding, and beer-drinking wire of a man who cursed frequently and said extremely questionable things about the opposite sex. He couldn't understand a word I was saying and the lack of comprehension was mutual. He was impressed, though, with my reference from the Brosna Press. It sealed the deal and I started the next day. The work was easy: I printed letterheads, invoice books, and the occasional complicated job like a colour prospectus for the local golf club or a book release. Other than that it was gravy. I started at seven thirty and finished at three thirty. It was ten minutes on my skateboard from the house. The first time I worked overtime—which we would come to do regularly—Mark F. arrived with a beer in his hand for me. This was a new experience for me—drinking while you work. Let's just say I started doing a lot of overtime. I had two co-workers, Mike and Steve, who loved the same music I did and also

Shaft of Light

loved getting drunk together. If I was to pick a point where alcohol really seeped into my blood, it was then in 1999. My old drinking habits had been mere flirtation up to this point. In Australia, I honed my ability to consume alcohol like a pro and functioned even better under its influence than when sober. The heat was insane and after our regular work hours it was either stay and get paid for drinking, or take Steve's car to the beach and hang out with his brother's friends. I was making what was for me a fortune, so we never stayed home. Restaurants, bars, strip clubs, VIP nights, you name it, we hit it. I didn't care when I got to bed. Often I'd get into work at six A.M., straight from a bar or the beach, and curl up on a chair for an hour before getting stuck into my printing quota for the day. Denise's death had made me feel like I was bullet-proof and I was always taking risks. I'd go for a midnight swim with groups of friends so drunk that I, too, could have drowned. I didn't have a desire to die, I just felt invincible. Until one day, when I was skating with Laura's boyfriend Mark and his friends. I came out of the lip of the bowl too high and tumbled down the side, breaking the scaphoid bone in my left wrist. The boss chewed me out for being reckless, but I didn't give a crap. It was two weeks before Christmas, so I packed my bags and took a train to Sydney. Three months before my arrival in Australia, there had been an exodus from Carrick on Shannon, Co Leitrim. Many people I knew from the weekends I spent in Carrick had, like me, moved to Australia

The Second Lap

on a one-year visa. Among them, two of my best friends, Himbob and Keck, were sharing a house with about fifteen Irish guys and gals.

That Christmas in Sydney was carnage. I lazed around with my wrapped up wrist on the receiving end of an endless beer supply and supermarket-sized bags of weed. I drank, smoked, and ate. On Christmas morning we did secret Santa and exchanged gifts. A few pipes were unwrapped and not being ones to stand on ceremony, we got high at breakfast. The guys had organised a huge lunch and we were seriously hungry by the time it was served. Eating turkey and Brussels sprouts in twenty-seven degree Celsius heat and then hitting the beach in swimming trunks and Santa hats drew zero complaints from me. Bondi Beach was crammed with plenty of fair skinned Irish that day, but I didn't feel one bit homesick. For the New Millennium Year I washed down a pile of ecstasy with a few litres of vodka and Red Bull and raved into the night at the Opera House. Stumbling wide-eyed into a bar the next morning to catch the Irish New Year on a TV screen, I was a wreck. I'm not sure what transpired there, but words were exchanged between me and some macho douchebag before he grabbed me by the scruff of the neck and threw me out on the pavement. I said goodbye to my buddies two days later and took the train back to Melbourne. I had to get back to work. My hand had healed after a four-week break, and I needed money. I'd been blowing cash all over the place. The drinking escalated on my return and

Shaft of Light

I could tell that Laura was worried. I partied harder and harder, sleeping with random women whom I met in bars or strip clubs. On occasion I'd wake up beside some girl and wonder where I was and how far it was to the nearest train station so I could get to work. If I knew her name, it was a bonus. In those days, as soon as I opened my mouth and women heard my accent, it was just too easy. I had always been a monogamous sort of person, but here I was living the dream! Some dream though because I didn't really feel anything. I was searching for something inside, but all I got was white noise. I hated the guy I was becoming.

After three months, Himbob came to live with me for a while, and I levelled out a bit. Keck and his girl Donna were in the city now too. One day after getting back from work, I found an envelope addressed to me from Carmel. Inside was the eulogy she had written for Denise, along with the music Denise had chosen for her funeral. I took the package to my room and sat on the floor. As I read Carmel's words whilst listening to Nick Cave and Cat Stevens, I broke down. I clutched the eulogy to my chest and lay in the foetal position screaming out sobs and barely able to catch my breath. I had been masking a sea of pain with my nonchalant persona. I feared facing up to how I felt about Denise's suicide because I knew when that wave broke, it would rough me up really good. I wailed until every tear had been wrung out of me. Physically exhausted, I lay there spent, exorcised almost. That night Himbob, Keck,

The Second Lap

Donna, Mike, and I went to a pub and toasted Denise. I finally had a chance to talk aloud with friends about her and to laugh instead of bottling all my pain up. Sometimes you just have to make peace within yourself and let go of the anger.

The friendships and experiences of Melbourne were hard to leave, but I had travelling to do. Laura and Aileen went home and I stayed with Mark for two weeks before heading on the road for four months. I love Melbourne and its vibrant underground culture. Leaving after just over half a year there, for me, it remains unspoiled.

Back in Sydney, I passed a week with Himbob and his crew; he'd had no luck finding work in Melbourne so he went back to his old job there. He was a bar manager and that afforded me the privilege of drinking a lot of free beer. Even so, Sydney and me never quite hit it off, and I was glad to leave again. Byron Bay was next and it was a hippie paradise. I stayed at a hostel called the Arts Factory where I played volleyball, bongos, and smoked dope. The nights would be passed walking on the beach listening to Bill Hicks in my headphones, the waves crashing in the background and the sand massaging my toes. The lighthouse there is at the most easterly point of the country and had a meditative quality to it. I felt serene there and glad to have the lights of the city in my rear-view mirror. Himbob joined me and for the next two and a half months, he became my travelling partner. I couldn't have been any luckier. He was mellow, and we loved the same

Shaft of Light

things; we would voraciously read books and swap them between ourselves. We did the famous Fraser Island trip with a group of seven in a four-wheel drive, camping under the stars every night.

Once, a dingo stole my camera from the tent and I chased him down the beach in my boxer shorts at sunrise. The camera had teeth marks on it and became known as the 'dingo cam'. We sailed the Whitsunday Islands and scuba dived on the Great Barrier Reef. If there is an Eden on earth, then that was it. I was in love with just being alive. Sometimes I would cry because I could not believe my luck that I had been given this opportunity. I filled journals and thought outside the box without needing LSD or magic mushrooms. I was unearthing my own vision of life and my part in it. Some of it was the romance of being on holiday, but being there did shape for me a more positive and broad-minded view of everything. The tour rolled north, the days filled with new towns, new faces and infinite possibilities.

5

Scraping the Sky

CAIRNS ENDED UP being my final destination, the town I would fly out of to go home. It was fitting as it gave me the sense of having come full circle. I had five weeks left. I'd asked around as to where the best hostel was and a guy who I'd met along the way and trusted said the Calypso Inn was groovy. Even though it was slightly out of town, it had a sweet little bar at the back which made it worth the walk. Himbob and I settled in really well. Cairns itself is a nice place, only the stinking humidity was on the rise. It was late September and the locals talked of how November was a killer with dead air and nightly tropical storms. The backpackers I met were all down to earth and not at all like the people I had encountered in the cities. They had trekked this far up north, and some

Scraping the Sky

of them would go further towards the rainforest afterwards. Himbob and I spent the first few days wandering around and checking out different bars, most of them replicas of Irish or English pubs with a good variety and quality of beers. The faux wooden interiors looked the same as every other Irish bar in the world, but as long as the staff were friendly, the beer cold, and the air conditioning cranked, we didn't care. I still had some money from my job to blow and planned a week of adventure. I went to the desk at the hostel and booked two things I had always wanted to do: bungee jump and skydive. On the day of the sky dive, I took off early from the hostel to catch the bus into town. I was absolutely the most nervous I'd ever been in my life. You see, I hate heights. Why does a guy who can't bear even to get up on a ladder decide to jump twelve thousand feet out of a plane attached only to a glorified bed sheet? The same reason I do most of the things in life, a seed is planted in my head and grows until I can't back out of it, much like this book really. I did a tandem jump, as to do a solo took three days of training and a lot more money. My tandem guy was a short German chap with a name that went in one ear and out the other.

"Don't worry, we haven't lost anyone this week," was his first comment. Funny guy. Who said the Germans have no sense of humour? He gave me the spiel about having been in the army and done hundreds of jumps. Then he instructed me what to do both in the plane and outside of it. The landing

The Second Lap

strategy was last on the list. It was simple really: we would rock three times when the plane door was opened, back, forward, back and then out. Once free falling, arms and legs had to be spread to make an X out of the body and the head tilted up. For the touchdown, I had to raise my legs and he would hit the earth first and then I could stand up. When I saw the plane, I nearly had a seizure. It was a thimble with two propellers, and it was going to take ten of us up on this suicide mission. As we climbed, Chuckles would show me the altitude gauge on his watch and when we got to eight thousand feet, already way too high, we still had four more to go. At twelve thousand feet, it looks like it does from the window of a Boeing, cars are dots and houses are matchboxes, only it feels more real and more dangerous in the *thimble*. When the door opened, Chuckles edged my butt out little by little until my right foot was resting on the wheel—the *wheel!* My heart was thundering and I could feel the wind pummelling my cheeks. Before I had time even to contemplate this utter insanity I had volunteered and *paid* for, he gave the three count. Back, forward, back and out......my body spun violently and I could see rapid flashes of sky and earth merge into a blue blur. Chuckles then got us settled into our free fall which was like taking all the drugs I had done before in my life in one dose and then shooting me from a canon. After forty seconds, he launched the parachute and we were delivered to the ground like soaring eagles. I had been keeping my legs up as I was told to do,

Scraping the Sky

but on the approach they were getting tired. Just as we were about to pull off the perfect landing, I put my long legs down and stumbled as Chuckles jolted forward unexpectedly and landed on my back. Once he disconnected us and peeled himself off me, I jumped around the field like a mad man. This was a rush beyond all! That night I got drunk and slept better than ever before.

The next day I went to the local tattoo parlour which was called FNQ Tattoo and run by legendary tattooist, Duane Cash. A girl I met on a sailing trip sported some of his artistry and said he was *the* guy to go to if I wanted to get inked. I'd had a tattoo done for my sixteenth birthday with my buddy, Poochie, back in the day after a hefty dose of cider. Mine was a modest Red Hot Chili Peppers asterisk, but Poochie couldn't help himself and got branded with a naked hooker in cowboy boots that covered a quarter of his back. For my Australian tattoo, I decided on Chinese characters that translated to the words 'sincere heart, sincere mind.' It would be a milestone for the times I had been through and even now, every time I look at it, I am reminded that's what I have to try to be. My first visit to FNQ, Duane wasn't around and his guys suggested I come back the next day. When Duane himself sat down in front of me to do it, I knew it was a good omen. His work stands head and shoulders above other tattooists in the care and time he puts into it. Himbob arrived mid-session to tease and take pictures. When the *pièce de résistance* was finished, I went straight out and rested my fresh ink on a bar

The Second Lap

counter and ordered some beers to get psyched up for the following day. Bungee jumping!

In early 1987, a New Zealander named AJ Hackett was in France with some friends and one single objective: find some high places to bungee from. Inspired by the Vanautu natives who jumped from thirty metre platforms with vines attached to their ankles as a rite of passage, Hackett wanted to take it further. After spending months in the Savoie region experimenting and testing the safety of the cords, he returned to Paris and set his sights on a jump that would change his life and the world of extreme sports. On a cool June evening, his team covertly smuggled the required amount of gear up one of the most iconic structures in the world—The Eiffel Tower. At dusk the next morning, having barely slept, Hackett took the plunge. The resulting media solidified his legend and commercial bungee was born. In 2000 when I was going to do my jump, there were sites in Queenstown, New Zealand, and Cairns, Australia. As I write, 'AJ Hackett Bungy' has sites in six countries, and through assorted gravity-related experiences has thrilled (or frightened the daylights out of) over three and a half million people. I chose Cairns.

The Cairns tower is situated fifteen km from the town at the foothills of Saddleback Mountain and stands a jaw-dropping fifty metres above a five-metre-deep pool. It's thirty metres wide at the base with two giant supports that taper to fifteen metres wide at the top where the jumping platform

Scraping the Sky

is, a daunting green metal structure that instills both fear and respect from the minute you first set eyes on it. At the weigh-in, you are asked whether you want to touch the water or not. On account of my fresh tattoo, I opted not to. I would, however, buy the photo package and video which in those days was VHS. The most discouraging part of the jump for me was the death march—six stories of winding steps that tied my stomach in knots. It was potentially easier to back out of than the sky dive was. Once I was in the plane, it was going to happen; if I chickened out here, all I had to do was walk back down to the comfort of the café below. So upward I went, occasionally peering below and vomiting my guts up. Reaching the top, I was greeted by a burly, bald-headed dude with a goatee. He laughed when he saw my fear. Sitting me down he wrapped my feet in a towel making sure it was comfortable between my ankles. He then placed a belt around the towel and secured it to the giant elastic that was going to keep me from a watery grave. Checking my weight which had been written on my left hand, he adjusted the tensile strength of the device and walked me to the edge. I stood there for what felt like half an hour, my heels balancing on the lip of the diving platform. There was no Chuckles there to push or encourage me, just my own willpower and the tiny looking pond below, a hundred and sixty feet of stretchy rubber between us. Then, everything went quiet; I emptied my mind and jumped. No worries.

The Second Lap

It is a very different experience than jumping out of a plane. The sheer height of a sky dive makes it almost unbelievable at the start. The ground is so far away it comes at you over a longer period of time. With bungee jumping you get the wind in your hair, too, but the ground is coming at you so fast that you close your eyes and pray that the cord whips you back up. It is a more compact burst of intensity, but both are some of the greatest forms of exhilaration I have experienced in my life.

My last and totally unplanned activity was rolling back into the tattoo studio for a lip piercing. I had been hanging out with a really sweet German girl named Anna whom I'd met on a sailing trip a few weeks before. She planned to get her tongue pierced. We made a deal to do it together. No stranger to piercings having had my nose, ears, and nipples pierced in the past, I was *the man* walking in there, but sweet Anna was extremely nervous. We sat in a sterile room with the air-conditioning on full. The contrast between the cold air and the humidity outside made me feel a little off balance but hey, I was an adventurer; this would be a cake-walk. Anna's piercing went without a hitch, and she was proudly sticking her swollen tongue out at me as the guy pulled a gleaming needle out of a cabinet drawer. I felt the cool steel puncture my right lip and my legs went dead. Putting the ring in, I could feel every drop of blood drain from my face. By the time he had it in I was lying on the table wishing I'd never been born. Anna laughed, I passed out.

Scraping the Sky

Once I got my feet under me, we went to a bar to celebrate.

Leaps from high places and piercings complete, I settled in for my last four weeks in Australia. I was really starting to become a part of the family at the hostel and they gave me a job sweeping the floors outside every morning from seven to nine. It was free board and easy work and I liked being up earlier when the temperature was cooler. Himbob had gone back to Sydney for his last week before returning home to Ireland, so I would see out my time there with all my English friends who had taken over the place. Weekends at the hostel were pumping with DJs and bands. Staff got beers for half price. Every evening we would roll up to eat at seven and then hit the pool table. I would drink a full case of beer with the chef, Reuben, and then when the cue sticks were put away I'd crash on our little couch on the balcony, smoking weed until the sun came up. I'd grab an hour or two of sleep and then do my sweeping before me and my new buddy Rob would drive to the airport to pick up the *newbies*. Most of them had just landed in Australia, wide-eyed with wonderment. We were always stoned, asking them all sorts of questions and making them feel as welcome as possible. I bared a very close resemblance to a late 90s version of the Woodstock generation. My long hair had started to grow into dread-locks, and even though I wasn't ready to join a commune, I felt a real contentment in our communal-like hostel.

The Second Lap

Then I met Marcella, and I couldn't breathe. She was a thin, tanned, fairy of a girl with chestnut eyes and skin like satin. She worked at the hostel too and had been in Australia for a year. German born with an Australian background, she had an accent that was hard to place. It didn't have the hard edge of German or the twang of Australian, more of a purr really. I was sick with butterflies the first time I saw her and her shyness only made her vulnerability more attractive. We played pool and flirted, but I assumed there was no possible way an angel like her would be interested in a barefooted barfly like me. Turns out I was wrong.

Tuesday night was cheap drinks night at the local sports bar. Shots and pints were knocked back with reckless abandon and the place was an absolute den of iniquity. I was feeling merry and not fully toasted when Marcella's friends approached me and said that she was leaving. She had gotten tired of waiting for me to make my move. *What?* I bolted from my seat and ran after her as fast as I could. My heart was leaping as I exited the bar and entered the balmy night air. I shouted out in the darkness after her and turning left, I saw her ambling across the park where I had seen her a few days beforehand with a friend. Sprinting barefoot with every ounce of effort, I caught up with her at the centre of the green, the moonlight casting her incandescent face just perfectly. She looked at me with those eyes and I took her in my arms and kissed her passionately. I think I even levitated a little, such was the sheer

Scraping the Sky

force of the feelings inside me. All she said was, "What took you so long, Paddy?"

That night we retreated to the balcony sofa that a select few of us used or even knew about. We smoked cigarettes, cuddled, kissed, and just stared into each other's eyes with an absolute certainty that at that moment not another soul existed in the universe. I woke to find her head on my lap, the soundtrack of stirring hostel bodies in the background as another day dawned in paradise. We quickly became a real couple. There was never talk of what would happen when we parted. We were not mushy or a couple who needed to be together all the time, but we loved sharing our lives with each other. We had a common group of friends and saw each other when we saw each other. One Thursday night as I walked her home, she turned to me and told me to meet her the next morning with my bags packed. I was intrigued and found myself a replacement sweeper for the weekend. Marcella had hired a car and was taking me to a remote Eco-friendly lodge in the heart of the rainforest. First we had to drive an hour to our destination and down a rickety old road where we parked. Then she rang a buzzer at a wooden gate and fifteen minutes later a man came to collect us in a Land Rover. He was quite young and explained to us that he and his wife had realised their dream by building the entire community mostly by themselves. It had a main restaurant and bar area that looked out over the huts. The bar exit led to a wooden platform suspended high above the forest

The Second Lap

floor that branched off in many directions. Each hut was at the end of a single walkway with tiny light-bulbs to guide the way. Ours was nestled on top of a ridge on the rainforest edge and boasted a spectacular valley and rolling green countryside views. Our entire surroundings blended in naturally. It was what I imagined heaven to be. We dined by candlelight, our soundtrack provided by the abundance of creatures whizzing through the night. I could not believe the kindness of the gesture and the way it made me feel—not only about her but about myself too. A person I so obviously cared for had gone to the trouble of organising this for a guy she had barely known two weeks. I hoped she didn't take all the guys here. After supper we made our way along the wooden path high up in the trees to our modest shack, and as I held her and kissed her that night, I knew I loved her. If time flies when you are having fun, then it vanishes like an extinguished candle flame when you are besotted. Sunsets seamlessly meshed into sunrises, our bodies entwined as we greeted each new day together, knowing it was one day closer to the end. Our weekend alone was the torch that ignited a burning love affair, after that we were inseparable. The end came three weeks later. Denial is a powerful thing, and as I lay in a heap at the airport at five o'clock in the morning, I thought I would pass out from the sadness. The last thing I saw was her head turn around one last time as she passed through the departure gate. A thousand emotions ran through me and my mind replayed

Scraping the Sky

every single second we'd spent together since our first kiss under the stars. The look in her eyes and her timid smile were like a dagger in my heart. Never again would I kiss her lips or feel her warmth each morning, nor would her laugh, her smell, or her touch intoxicate my senses.

When we said good-bye, something inside me broke. Fate parted us and we never promised to stay in touch or to try to take it any further; it would have been too painful for either of us. A holiday romance had turned into the greatest love my life had ever known. She just *got* me, she never tried to change me or be anyone but herself in my presence. She loved not only the good things about me but also the faults. Is it possible we could have burned on as brightly? Maybe not. I hope she is happy now, thirteen years later, and maybe has a family of her own and a husband who thinks the sun rises and falls with her. Whenever I think of her, I am grateful to have known her.

People often ask me about Australia out of their own curiosity and after I've recounted the great times I had there, I'm met with the same question, "Why did you come back?" The answer is quite succinct—I had changed and I presumed the friends and people I'd left behind for a year had too. For thirty hours on my way home, I pondered a year's worth of living and where I would go from here.

I landed in London with ten dollars in my pocket. It was just enough to change into sterling and place a call to Mark and Laura to tell them I

The Second Lap

was on my last layover. An hour later I hopped on a plane to Dublin and found them waiting for me when I landed. They drove me home to the sleepy village of Cloghan, dropping me at the town square with my bag on my back. Heavily bearded, tattooed, pierced lip, and with shoulder-length hair, I walked passed St. Mary's school and in the front gates of my parents' yard. My dad was sitting in his usual chair looking out the window. He leapt up, shouting that Mally was home. A surge of brothers and sisters came running out the back door to hug me and welcome me back. It was wonderful to see them. I spent the next week getting together with friends.

After four days all the family stuff was out of the way and I had recovered enough from jet-lag to make the trip to Galway to visit Denise's grave. I stayed at the girls' apartment the day before as we had so much to talk about. They gave me a big joint and her suicide note and left me alone in a room for twenty minutes. I read with trepidation and inhaled the smoke deeply, holding in my hands the last thing she had ever written. In the letter, she apologised to me and others for what she had done and why she had done it. The following day we made the drive further west to her grave. It was painful, but I had wrung out most of my grief that emotional day in Melbourne. Around her final resting place we made jokes and remembered her spirit during her brief life. Since Denise's death I have known too many people who have taken their own lives. I know the devastation and questions it leaves behind; I also

Scraping the Sky

know that the overwhelming urge to take my own life some years later gave me an insight into how helpless life can sometimes feel.

I returned to my old job at the Brosna Press the next week and made a much-needed visit to the hair salon to have my crusty dread-locks chopped off. The lip ring stayed, for a while at least.

I foolishly thought that because of my Australian experience, and the way I'd matured and developed as a person, that my mates back in Ireland would have been on a similar path. But the same guys sat on the same bar stools talking the same crap they were spouting the year before. I was horrified. How was I supposed to live through this—having changed so much—and not lose my mind?

I started to drink with a fundamental shift in my attitude towards alcohol. I was no longer drinking to have a good time; I was drinking to escape. I would go to the pub for a beer one evening a week after work, then two, and then three until it was almost every day. If it wasn't a pub, it was a friend's house to smoke hash and knock back cans of whatever was being passed around. Getting up in the morning became harder, not because of the physical effects of the booze yet, but because I didn't want to. I could scarcely muster the enthusiasm to crawl out of the mental fog that clouded my vision. At noon on Sundays, I would go to the pub, drink ten pints of Guinness and then come home and write. After that it was nap time and dinner before

The Second Lap

round two. It took another five or six pints just to get me to sleep.

Meanwhile, my mate Trev had some news of his own. The girl he had been seeing for a few years had moved to London and he was following her. I was pleased for him and told him so. He was gone by the summer. The night before he left, we went drinking at a local pub. I was so emotional over our beers that I told him I was going to the toilet and snuck out the back door. I hate good-byes, always have. He settled well and we talked a couple of times a month, the same as we had whilst I was down under. We wrote letters, but I missed him. I was miserable. What else could I do? Stay in the same town, smoking pot out the back of a shed and pretending my life was OK? Trev was gone; I was stuck back home and piteous after a year of the high life.

Drinking one Sunday afternoon at my favourite pub, I was wasted by four o'clock in the afternoon when all the local football studs came in after a game. I sat there with a suppressed contempt for them, the town, the mindset, everything. I didn't belong here and this was not part of the plan. If the Everest of my life had been scaled, I was now on my backside and flying down the mountain with no brakes. That day I wobbled home and called Trev's number only for his girlfriend to answer. She was as hammered as I was and I told her of my frustration and anger at being trapped. Her suggestion was that I move to London. That sounded like a good idea to me. With the cogs of our minds sufficiently lubricated,

Scraping the Sky

a plan was hatched to help me flee Nowheresville. I popped my head into the kitchen and told my parents in a slur that I was moving to London. They weren't surprised, but thought it was just the alcohol talking. That Monday morning, I jumped out of bed with vigour, my mind made up. I was going back to tell Brownie, yet again, that I was leaving, this time for good.

In London, Trev was jumping up and down with joy. They decided to get a bigger place with a room for me. I wired over a deposit and some rent money to hold the room and started packing my bags. It was a week after I'd decided to move and eight months since I'd been back from Oz and all I had was a plane ticket and some clothes in a bag. The next part of the adventure was about to begin. No crystal ball told me what was going to happen. The ten years that followed changed my life irrevocably and is the main reason this book is in your hands. I had been on the roller coaster for a while with partying and living it large, only this time the ride got even bigger and badder, and I was not strapped in. The drugs would be more potent, the highs and lows more extreme, and a maelstrom of self-loathing would eventually inhabit the guy whom I once knew and cared about, me.

Me! It had been so long since I had thought about me and my life growing up in Ireland. Through all the drugs and booze, if I concentrated really hard, I could actually remember those idyllic days which had so strongly imprinted both the good and bad

The Second Lap

traits of my life. Staring blankly out the window of the plane, I fell into reviewing my past as I flew over the Irish sea towards England. Having reconnected with family and friends, I had deep thoughts about the importance of my childhood.

6

Roots

I VAGUELY RECALLED being in an upstairs bedroom of our two-storey house in Banagher, Co Offaly, at age, if I was to hazard a guess, three. I was with my older sister Susan and we were drawing pictures in some new colouring books. I had lost my pencil sharpener under a roll of carpet (or maybe it was linoleum) that was lying heaped in a corner, and I was obsessed about retrieving it. The not knowing where it was actually annoyed me more than any need to sharpen pencils, a mild OCD tic that still irks me to this day. When I ask sister Susan about this, she always responds the same, "I don't know what the hell you're on about." On first impressions though, life seemed pretty good. I liked it. What was not to like? I had a wonderful older sister who taught me things and my next door

The Second Lap

neighbour, John, was the first best friend I had. John and I were inseparable and over time we would go exploring, running off to the sports ground to hide in hollowed-out trees, or take our walkie-talkies and go on missions to the fields far away. The field was actually across the road, but in our minds it seemed far away. Possibly the greatest thing about being a kid is that everything seems so huge and mysterious. No worries about rent or children or the freedom to not be influenced by much other than whose football album had the most stickers in it. John felt like a brother to me and our bond was based on a camaraderie that inspired all the great friendships I have been blessed to have over the years. The people I hold close are not necessarily people I see all the time, but an appreciation for the time we *do* spend together bridges the gaps in between and creates not just memories, but lifetime memories. I understood loyalty from the very start—when I am with you, I am *totally* with you.

Just a three minute walk up the road from our house was my first classroom in an aged building that screamed dullness and routine. It was horrible—weeds and grass pushed through cracked tarmac; moss grew on the rectangular, slabbed exterior. When I crossed the threshold, the first bell that rang was the one in my head telling me I didn't belong in pre-school. The freedom of our yard where I ran around with our dog, Mason, playing fetch, was where I belonged, not stuck in some room with a bunch of others being told what to do. I despised

Roots

the woman who watched over me at every turn. I always felt like it was as if something or someone was just waiting for me to mess up—waiting to pounce. My parents were not strict. Only when I reached the age of six or seven and started seeking attention through thieving, did I get into bother with them. Now, there are so many clinical definitions for children with attention-related disorders. Then, it was more black and white. If a kid misbehaved, they were put in line (and not by a child psychologist). As I settled into my 'prison,' I discovered there were better ways to pass the time, like saying things I shouldn't and generally getting noticed for all the wrong reasons; stealing from others, fighting, and acting like Charles Bronson (my father was a big fan). Was I in for a shock in primary school! The sheer scale of the change was like landing on another planet—the teachers were alien and the air so thin, I couldn't breathe!

I got into plenty of trouble in primary school for the same reason—the desire for attention. I was a jealous kid, full of rage if someone came into class with a new school bag or a shiny pencil case better than mine. One day, I stood looking in the window of Flynn's, the local general store. I stood and I stood, utterly transfixed by a pair of Superman sneakers staring out at me from the window display. Their snappy Velcro fasteners and giant red, blue, and yellow triangular logo looked so cool that I imagined slipping them on and flying away. One day my friend Dessie entered the classroom wearing

The Second Lap

them. Dessie was a great friend throughout many playground sessions and football games. But when *he* came in with *my* shoes on *his* feet, I saw red, rag-to-a-bull-red. I didn't react straight away. I was tactical. I wanted him to know I wasn't happy in the most attention-gathering manner possible. Lunch time! As kids ran outside and between corridors, I seized my chance. Dessie was on the other side of a wooden door with square glass panels from midway up. I charged at the door, fuelled by the need to make it known to the world that those shoes I coveted so dearly were now in the possession of someone else. The sensation when my head crashed through that glass panel I have come to know again and again. Only now I get that same release from forty km trail runs. I got my point across. I got noticed. Three stitches in the top of my skull later, I had acquired a reputation as a loose cannon that would do anything to be seen on the world's radar. Little did I know that our days in Banagher were numbered. At the age of five and having done my year in the junior infants class, our family packed up. I would have to leave my classmates and leave Mrs. Hughes, who in spite of being an alien in this other world seemed a nice woman in my young eyes. I was crushed. Things were falling into place; I was more at ease, my temper calming, and we were leaving. Not just our home, but playmates too. I would have to find a new best friend. It was about to begin all over again.

7

Against

MY FATHER, JOHN, hailed from Cloghan, a neighbouring town roughly eight km away from Banagher—it was more rural. Being a new boy in a small village in Ireland, or probably anywhere, is an invitation to be mocked. Our new house was beside the family home where my dad grew up in a large Catholic family—we're talking double figures here. Each son and daughter spread out over the country with their own families; I had numerous cousins whom I never saw. The town was smaller and less populated, but it did have more green. Our newly-assembled, prefabricated house backed onto fields that rolled on as far as the eye could see. This was my new playground. Suddenly things didn't seem so bad. At least my surroundings didn't seem so bad.

The Second Lap

My dad and my grandfather Kieran argued a lot, shouting at each other over the fence that divided his house and our house. The swearing they exchanged at times scared me a little. My dad's fuse was short, but his quick temper was also short-lived. When he lost his cool, it was over before you even knew it started. Employed by the Electricity Supply Board (ESB) at Ferbane Power Station, he worked as a sampler in the laboratory where he tested soil and other variables to determine the earth's moisture. The ESB was the main source of power throughout the country and was the biggest employer in the area. The men there worked hard, smoked hard, and drank hard. I loved when he would take me in for an afternoon. The various science accoutrements that lined the desks and cabinets mesmerised me. Beakers, tubes and all sorts of measuring equipment in this grown-up world made me proud my father worked here. I couldn't wait to boast of all these things I had seen at school. I could easily win any "My dad has a better job than your dad" argument when the occasion presented itself.

The change of schools, however, was completely demoralising. I acutely remember my introduction to bullying. It was my first day, and I was the new kid. I was so timid and afraid that I thought I'd wet my pants. The boys seemed bigger, and unlike my old school, there were no girls. When the boys in the grade above mine—who shared our class's classroom—looked at me, I could see what they saw: they were eyeing their new punching bag. I

Against

was sitting at my desk—shy and scared, and this kid named Paddy looks over at my school bag—a Liverpool soccer club bag. I didn't know a thing about soccer; I just had the bag, which my mother had probably purchased because it was the cheapest one available. Paddy, however, already had a passion for the sport. He decides to take it on himself to tell me that Liverpool was, in fact, "useless." Uh, OK. This though was the tip of the iceberg as far as bullying incidents were concerned. Our school, St. Mary's, was a breeding ground for fighting and disrespect and had a hierarchy that seemed to stem from two things: your family background and the church. Small villages in Ireland have a pecking order. Most towns the world over probably do as well where one is ranked by lineage, class, or relationship to those in authority. Cloghan was a town of GAA footballers. If you were a good player and came from a family who had a long-standing history within the town, then you were set. One group of kids suffers, the other flourishes. The good players received preferential treatment in the classroom. A select group of boys had the privilege of making the tea for the *master* at eleven o'clock break time. They were responsible for boiling the kettle and getting biscuits. From my vantage point, the tea makers strutted around with the air of superiority that their status afforded them. I was baffled at how the system worked. Why is the kid next to me who is from a poorer background, or has troubles at home because of a parent's illness or other misfortune, not allowed a chance to shine

The Second Lap

and feel important? I didn't blame the spoiled kids as much as their parents and the teachers. It's the way the world revolves. As I progressed through school, I decided that I too should be afforded the right to make tea.

It was a Friday morning. Reg, the kid who made the daily brew, was preparing to boil the kettle. I had other ideas. I got up just as Reg did, and made a bee line for the kettle. Mr. Nolan, a bear of a man with a propensity for lifting kids off the ground by the hairs on the back of their necks shouted at me, "McLoughlin, what in the blazes do you think you are doing?"

"Just making the tea, sir." At which point he laughs, tells me not to be so stupid and limply waves his hand to direct me back to where I 'belonged.' Tea making, it seemed, was not in my future.

A brief history

St. Mary's National School was a hundred yards from our house on Castle Street. It was said a castle once existed on our street, but that's all historical conjecture that I won't investigate here. The school was a long flat rectangle of a building that had a lawn out front, a basketball court out back and the lamest excuse for a football pitch I'd ever seen. It was split in two: the left side had three classrooms for the boys and the right side, which mirrored the left in size and shape, was for the girls. This arrangement was good in a way—we boys saw the girls at break times and lunch times. Couples paired off and had romances,

Against

of a sort; when I say romance, I mean lust that is transferred into throwing snowballs at the one you fancy or chasing after them in a game of tag. I laugh at the naivety now but am also moved by the purity of it all. Marian was my first girlfriend—gorgeous Marian—sweet, kind. One Easter she gave me a big red Easter egg all wrapped up with a card attached. I was blasé. I was too cool. Innocent times. It amazes me now—the footprints of the people we become and the adult relationships we end up having are imprinted in our youth. Of course, the relationships worked like the football team: if you were cool, the hot girl with the well-known parents noticed you. But I didn't care. I had Marian and I had my supply of chocolate eggs and that was all I needed. I would daydream about her constantly during class. There was never any kissing, just the occasional holding of hands. And she was the best looking of all the girls, of course.

The teachers on the boys' side were Mrs. Mahoney, Mr. Kelly, and Mr. Nolan. Mr. Nolan, or Yogi Bear as he was known, was the principal. The teaching methods of each one varied and were, by today's standards, unorthodox. However, I remember learning so much from each one that to this day, I am grateful for their input and personalities. Mrs. Mahoney taught first and second class. She was not a huge pusher regarding conventional school work—she loved poetry and drama, and other artistic, creative expressions. She was tough, but I saw in her a woman who cared and did her absolute best

The Second Lap

for us all. She would organise these poetry readings that everyone had to participate in, getting up and reading wasn't enough. It had to be a performance piece recited from memory and the more dramatic it was, the greater her praise. Having an innate flair for the spectacular, I always set the bar higher than the rest. After her came Mr. Kelly, the tallest man I had ever seen, who had a temper that, like my father's, came at you with no advance warning. Case study one: chatting incessantly to a classmate on a Friday afternoon when this metre stick—a long ruler used for marking lines on the board or flailing the living daylights out of kids like me—landed on my hand like a guillotine. The throbbing sting was followed by silence. He looked at me without saying anything; the ruler did the talking. Case study two: I was, yet again, being distracted, only this time it was with my new pen. I was so happy with it that all I could do was fiddle with it, clicking the button and flying it through the air as if it was a rocket splitting the sky. Which it did, right before it split wide open. As much as I was in a world of my own, Mr. Kelly was also in this world, and he didn't like what he saw. Again, and without warning, a slap from a hand as big and unbending as the head of a shovel connected with my left ear. The pen was thrown out an open window and smashed on impact with the basketball court below. The first pang was for my mother; she had bought me that pen. Not only was I afraid of her anger, I was more empathic about her disappointment in my behaviour—that she had

Against

gone to the trouble to provide things for me that a teacher could destroy.

And that teacher—did he have any idea that parents worked hard to pay for these things? Disciplinarian aside, he was very much on the button regarding my great passions: books, and spelling. Each Monday he would hand us a list of fifty or so words, followed by a test on Friday. I may have kicked a football like a newly born foal trying to stagger to its feet, but when it came to the spelling test, I was top dog! I studied hard every week and would settle for nothing less than 20/20. The best score came with a bonus: no homework for the weekend. I was pretty much on top of that for as long as I can remember. Until the day it became too much, the test done, our answers submitted. We normally had a few minutes to chat and chill and to look over our answers, but I quickly realised that I had gotten one wrong. I went into survival mode. I can't have the one thing I'm good at taken away from me so I have to find a way to amend it. I strolled nonchalantly up to the desk on the pretext of asking Mr. Kelly a question. My M.O. was to distract him long enough to change the word on my answer book. It was just the most amazing chance that the incorrect word was on a page that was hanging slightly downwards over the edge of his desk. I asked him something stupid and quickly changed the letter at the same time. When he read out the results I had won. It was what I wanted, but instead of elation, I felt nothing. I had cheated and it meant nada because

The Second Lap

I had not gotten the result under my own steam or effort. I learned a lesson that day that is still with me every time I feel like making a short cut in life.

Mr. Nolan's was next: the big league, fifth and sixth class. This was a new level and the tea making altar boys who had been hovering over us since the beginning were nearing the end of their term. They wouldn't leave without being kings of the school and we wouldn't be taken as a bunch of chumps either. Rivalry was fierce. We had a crew of courageous misfits, cheeky, smart, and with zero fear—David, Padraig, his brother John, Damien, Poochie, and myself. We took pleasure in being the underdogs and if you picked on one of us, you took us all on. They had been hanging crap on us for a few years. If Mr. Nolan happened to leave the class for five minutes, no opportunity was lost to throw a pen, ruler, or flick an elastic band or any other stationery that came to hand and could cause damage. We didn't play around, you got maybe one good shot and if you so happened to catch the guy who kicked you at the soccer ground the previous day unawares, then all the better for you. Not for him obviously. It was around this time in my life that religion came more into focus: it was the age of confirmation and many of the 'chosen few' in our class were also altar boys. I wasn't sure how one applied for such a prestigious position and more to the point, I didn't care. They got the benefit of occasionally leaving school at ten A.M. to serve mass. To me, it was conforming, just like the football and the tea making. Of course, the one

Against

great contradiction within me is that I have always been a spiritual sort of person; I just couldn't handle the preaching. Growing up in traditional Catholic Ireland was a really damaging experience for a lot of people. Most would never admit this, but looking back at how we were taught is like holding a mirror in front of society, the despair was a reflection of a country that had suffered so much hypocrisy and tried to sweep most of it under the carpet. I believed that God was with me, almost like an imaginary friend whom I could talk to whenever I needed one, more a spirit than a bearded man in the sky who would shove me off to hell for thinking about girls' breasts. Priests sermonised from up high on the pulpit with a superiority that seemed unreachable. I never felt the connection with the priests or the eight o'clock Saturday night mass. For me, it was about being in the fields on my own and having my one-on-one relationship with whoever happened to be listening. Those early days were the catalyst for a lot that followed in turbulent parts of my life. Religion was divisive. I'm an open-minded Christian and I don't preach; case closed. Religious organisations, on the other hand, are a whole different kettle of fish. I remember the day clearly when the bubble burst on it all. I was with Uncle Jim and Aunt Suzy on a drive somewhere and I think my cousin Ivan was there too. Suzy and Jim were glued to a radio program discussing 'sex abuse' and a priest. I didn't quite grasp the finer points of what was being said, but the tone of the presenter and his panel, coupled

The Second Lap

with the glances exchanged between my aunt and uncle told me that there was a storm brewing, and the storm was a biggie. From the memory I have of it now, this was the first sex scandal to go public. What followed was a flood of young boys coming forward with horrific stories of rape at the hands of priests. Nuns were next in the firing line for their beatings and ill treatment of girls at convents. Case after case, each one more disturbing than the previous, came to light and shocked the nation. But it didn't shock them enough. Damage control meant these priests never got the full justice they deserved. They were retired off somewhere, out of sight and out of mind. I may not remember too much about the aftermath of the whole scandal, but I remember that day like it was a few months ago. However, I was with my Aunt Suzy and Uncle Jim, so I felt safe. Uncle Jim was my mother's brother. Florence and Jim of Ballycumber, Co. Offaly, were the offspring of Annie and Denis and about a million miles removed from my father's family in both numbers and circumstance. The connection of all our family is almost a full circle as my parents met at the engagement party of Suzy and Jim. This bond with them has a deeper connection than most in the family would probably admit aloud. To me, it's special and we will always be inextricably intertwined because of many factors that have brought both tremendous joy and heartbreaking sadness.

8

Life Trails

GOING TO 'GRANNY'S' was always the best and most anticipated road trip. It was only eighteen km away, but it felt like a holiday on the weekends. It was the real countryside: a few neighbouring houses in the distance and a labyrinth of a forest out the back that rested on this big boulder which was probably there from the beginning of time. And just to pour some more gravy on top of this gravy, there was a *Bord na Mona* works adjacent to her brick cottage. Translation: it was bog and tractors and machinery and drains and rail tracks for what looked like infinity. It was an outdoor adventure land that was like Disneyland for me before I even knew about Disneyland. It was unadulterated freedom, and Suzy and Jim's kids were the same age as me and Susan. We had also been

The Second Lap

joined by the newest edition, Simon, who arrived five years after me. Now we were three. On our cousins' side, there were Sinéad, Ivan, and Greg, respectively, and our ages varied by mere months in some cases. We were close. My best memories are of playing hide and seek in the woods and going off on adventure trails uninhibited by boundaries. Susan and Sinéad did their thing, Ivan and I got into whatever trouble was closest at hand, and Simon and Greg were the youngest—not quite at the age of becoming a handful, not yet anyway. My recollections of my grandfather Denis are vague in general, but specific details or moments have surprising clarity. He was a tall man, with a craggy and distinctive face in a Samuel Beckett-type way, and did a lot of farming. To me, he was the biggest man I knew, and not just physically. His presence had superiority in a way, almost like he had seen and done things in life that you can't comprehend unless you have lived it. He would take Susan and I on tractor drives through hilly fields to check on the horses. The branches scraping the roof of the tractor cab was both terrifying and exciting. On these little adventures he would change the huge salt blocks hanging from the trees for the horses to lick. One day he let me touch one with my finger and taste it in order to try and explain better what it was for. It was not a nice taste, but I got a certain encouragement as a child from being trusted to try something as opposed to being told "no" all of the time. People say I get my height from him, and that pleases me because I did

Life Trails

not know him long enough to understand the finer points about him as a person. It was the saddest of days arriving at his stables with my parents and Susan to find him lying peacefully in the straw. It seemed so out of the ordinary even though I was only three years old at the time. He looked at peace, where he belonged, like an old animal who repairs to a private and comfortable place to pass on from this world. It was a brain haemorrhage, he died in the ambulance on his way to the hospital. How much he suffered I'll never know, but I do have a sense of peace knowing he was at a place he loved and where he spent so much of his time. I am proud of the fact that my middle name is his name.

Annie 'Granny' Mahon was and is a saint in my eyes. She influenced me in more ways than any human being on this earth. The words "find your happy place" were invented for homes like hers, and because of how young I was when my grandfather passed, it's Granny who stands head and shoulders above everyone else in shaping my life. She was a simple woman with a killer laugh. She would begin a story and crack up before she got to the end. Everyone would be hunched around waiting for the punch line that she was hysterically trying to deliver. Then, as is the way, everyone else lucky enough to be in the room would just start wailing laughing too. The punch line was never that funny, if she even made it that far. She had an ability to radiate warmth and light that I've not seen since. She made me feel there was someone on the earth just for me when

The Second Lap

times got rough. I just loved her purely and honestly. Her circle of friends in the village where she lived all her life in a modest bungalow was enormous. She loved playing bingo and had so much luck in winning that nobody could believe how fortunate she was. But angels have a way of being lucky. She always, always, always gave it back to her family or friends because that was her way. Ten year-olds have a hard time understanding the concept of money: I thought it grew on trees, unlimited supplies of it. She distilled everything to simplicity—that was the greatest thing about her; she showed me the way instead of telling me. I would do jobs for her like cutting timber, painting window ledges, and the many other tasks that need doing at a country house. My rewards were a few pounds here and there. The money was my pay to buy tapes and records which I started getting into, but I also felt pride in the job. She examined my work, pointing out if I missed a spot, or ribbing me for taking a short-cut; "if it was worth doing," she said, "it was worth doing right." Her approval meant the world and my effort reflected not the need for her blessing as much as the need for her to know that I did my best for her. I now know that this time in all our lives was purer and more unhurried than it ever would be again. There is a kaleidoscope of nostalgia in my mind that plays like an old movie reel whenever I see photos or pause to think about that period, because it was perfect.

The foundation of our very beings was irrevocably crushed, though, at a time when we least expected.

Life Trails

Actually saying 'least expected' is a bad joke. Never in the world did anyone *ever* envision that someone we adored would have to leave us and break our hearts forever. It haunts me more than I care to acknowledge because there is no justification for any family having to go through such pain. Trying to make sense of it as a child was no different than trying to make sense of it as an adult. It seems like a dream and that someday our lives will be woken from the nightmare of that day to find our darling, angelic girl smiling back at us. However, as beautiful as life can be it can also be the cruellest and most random of theatres. My recollection is of the small details that you normally don't notice, a day where everything had the intensity of looking through a magnifying glass and the information my eyes relayed is seared into every fibre of my brain. Attempting to keep it all behind the doors of the dark places, closed and locked out of sight, is futile. You can try to suppress it, but someday you just have to face it head on.

It was Saturday morning, September 3rd, 1988, and it started with excitement and an expectation of a weekend's freedom, but it ended tragically and unlike any other day in living memory. I got up and dressed and was heading over to Ivan's house to play for the day. He lived on the other side of the town and in order to go by car, it was a simple straight road for a few hundred metres, an acute right after the roundabout (called a *square* in Cloghan—which tells you all you need to know about the place) and then straight down another few hundred metres

The Second Lap

before swinging a right into a semi-circular terrace of houses. There was a large green for playing sports in front of the houses and summer time was a blitz of hurling, football, rugby, and American football as all the locals turned up to run themselves ragged. Even a small circus passed through from time to time over the years. But instead of having to take the footpath all the way around to Ivan's, it was much easier to go through the fields. Our front door faced their back yard with a distance of maybe three hundred metres; the only obstacle was a fence at the half-way point which was easily surmountable to a seasoned ditch hopper such as myself. After that it was a small drain at the end of the garden before hopping over the fence and *voilà*, playtime.

On this Saturday morning, however, something was different. When I arrived, something was very wrong with Sinéad. Suzy and Jim were not to be seen. The neighbours took both me and Ivan to their house, it was at a forty-five degree angle so we sat looking out through the neighbours' window with the innocence that only a child can have, and wondered to ourselves why the adults in the room conversed in whispers. People began arriving across the way. An ambulance came. The crew brought out a stretcher and entered the house. The tension rose to a heightened sense of cognisance that was difficult to fathom.

What's going on? was all that filled my head. *OK, something is up, but what?* Kids are not stupid. Keeping them in the dark doesn't help. They have

Life Trails

a highly sensitive gauge to adult stresses and behaviours.

After what seemed like an eternity, the ambulance crew reappeared with the stretcher—with someone on it, its rigid bars and metallic clank imparting an air of finality as they slid it into the back, closed and locked the door behind it, and then drove away. All of the events leading up to this one moment felt aggravated. I couldn't grasp how "sick" Sinéad was until I walked into their living room a few hours later. It was like walking into a wall of tears. Suzy was broken. Jim's eyes had changed from the warm windows they had always been to a vacant empty stare. My own mother sobbed convulsively as did everyone else in the room. I found my father and sat on his knee wondering how can a sick girl cause so much pain to those who love her?

"When will she get out of the hospital and come home?" I asked my father. I can still hear his voice now saying,

"Sinéad is dead; she had an accident and won't be coming home; she is in heaven now."

I folded over as every ounce of air left my body in a wail of confusion and sorrow. How can this be? She was my cousin and these things don't happen to our family. The McLoughlins and the Mahons are a team; we're all close in age, and we go to Granny's and play and get into trouble, and Susan and Sinéad.... and on and on and on; my head swirled. The desperate question of why this occurred I still ask today, and my answer is that she really was an

The Second Lap

angel, and this is how I will always see her. She had something ephemeral about her, like she was sent to show us all the true beauty within a person's soul. She burned fast and bright; she was a comet and her light shines through in all of us who remember her inner and outer beauty.

Sinéad had fallen in her room, a freak accident. She passed away from complications. There was no way to get her back. Hindsight can make you crazy if it gets under your skin, but everyone on hand that day did the best they could and that's as simple as it can be put. The sheer wave of grief and respect paid to her and her family testified to the privilege it was to have known her. I still feel her on my shoulder when things are not going my way, her aura as lucent as her life. There will never be another like her. She was only thirteen years old.

Days in Granny's were also a stark contrast to going back to Cloghan. There I felt increasingly alienated because at the time I was not sporty. In 1987, a cyclist named Stephen Roche changed that for me. Roche was a gutsy Dubliner who won the Giro d'Italia, Le Tour de France, and the World Championships—all in the same year. Only the legendary Eddy Mercx, considered to this day the greatest rider ever, had achieved this. Needless to say, I and many others were bike mad. I had a rust bucket on bent wheels with five gears, all of them useless. Unperturbed, I got involved in a local club that was beginning to blossom. Ivan had joined a few weeks before and talking to him at Granny's one

Life Trails

weekend, he told me of the outings of up to twenty people. This was a veritable *peloton,* (I was getting the lingo down too) and the thoughts of riding with them was keeping me awake at night. There was, and still is for me, something magical about a group of cyclists moving as one body, like a flight of swallows dancing through the air on a summer's evening. The fluidity and seamlessness of turning corners with just a few inches between wheels is almost a performance art. My first time waiting for the club to arrive at the roundabout in Cloghan was exhilarating. I was ready to go, and I was serious. I was on a jalopy, but sometimes it's not the song, it's the singer. The older experienced riders told stories and helped the younger ones out. I never remember feeling tired, only hypnotised by the sound of whirring wheels and the flashing colours of jerseys as they passed. Our loop may have only been twenty km, but I felt I had been given an insight as to what was beyond my front door. The greatest satisfaction was the ability to get to these places under my own steam. It was the beginning of one of the greatest passions of my life and an identity that brought some amazing friendships along the route. What I was also discovering about myself was this: when I got into something, I devoured it. I have a compulsion within me to have to know everything about my interest. Moderation is not something I have ever cared for and never will. I become consumed by my passions, sometimes to the detriment of myself and the others around me. I *cannot* help it. Some people

The Second Lap

call it an addictive personality, but that's not me. I'm obsessive. I've practised many things over the years. And, I don't entirely abandon my fixations; I just have a very intense phase of interest. Once I've mastered something, I move on.

Now I had a new interest and the first course of action was to exchange the piece of crap with a saddle. I begged my mother to get me a new bike. A word on my mother: Florence McLoughlin (née Mahon) is without a shadow of doubt her mother's daughter. A fair woman, but if you crossed her, then you best beware. My recollections of my youth and being around her taught me about being honest and being principled. One time during a local elections campaign, when the fat money-grabbing-crooked-as-a-coat-hanger politicians came to peoples' doors, they paid a visit to chez McLoughlin. Picture me as I peer out from around the door jamb of the living room to see who is taking a roasting from my mum for failing to deliver on promises and for not having the best interest of the village at heart. I was thinking to myself, *Hey, if you're not happy about something, then speak up*. It wasn't like she was berating the guy for no valid reason. She had points, and they were good ones. She was also a firm enforcer of the idea that life is not a free ride. My work ethic in every job I've ever had has been because of my mother and Gran.

On Saturday mornings for sure we'd hear Mum reminding us, "You aren't going anywhere this

Life Trails

morning until you help with chores! You know what to do."

Susan and I would look at each other as if we had never heard those instructions before in our lives, and then, mimicking mum, she'd add, "You take out the ashes from the fire; I'll dust." Whoever got done first would do the vacuuming. We just wanted to get out of there pronto. Sounds like child labour? It couldn't have been further from it. It showed us early on that we had responsibilities. Of all the things in the world I learned from her, I thank her for this above all. I am also ever grateful for her unwavering support of anything I ever did, and I did a lot. With cycling, it was decided that if I was serious I could withdraw the money from my post office savings account and buy a new MBK bike, the same make as Stephen Roche's. It was another move to show me the value of money and to give me independence. She dropped me outside the post office in Moate, Co Westmeath, and in I went alone, at age twelve. I asked the lady to give me £200. She was half laughing and half alarmed as to what to say to a kid who is just above the counter in height. After a little explaining that mum was outside, she decided to give me *my* money and I crossed the street to pick up my new machine. I was jumping like a jelly bean in anticipation of the following Sunday. I had new shorts, a new jersey, and a sleek new twelve speed. Rubber was going to be burned. I felt cocky and strong, and I had no issue with chasing after a twenty-year old guy. I just didn't care. You ride hard;

The Second Lap

I'll ride hard. It's difficult to quantify a predator instinct in a pre-teen kid. It wasn't so much a need to beat my chest and proclaim to be the greatest, for me, it was the need to better myself. Not to ride as fast as the others, but to ride as fast as *I* could, and to look back on having made a solid effort.

The cycling meetings started to take on a new life when our club decided it was time to create a series of mid-week league races. These races were held mostly on Wednesday evenings during the summer months. It was an opportunity for us to test our abilities in a very informal and friendly way. Each age group raced over an undulating loop of fifteen km, and it broke up the monotony of the week. The issues of school were nothing more than a mild distraction at this stage. I lived for the league races and the Sunday outings which grew in both distance and numbers. Again and again, the crux of the riding for me was about my own capabilities, testing myself against the unknown boundaries that I thought existed. One Wednesday on race night, our group encountered another bunch of cyclists out for a training ride. Athlone C.C. was a club from the neighbouring county. It was soon agreed that they too would be able to join and make the events more diverse and dare I say competitive. The first thing that struck me about these guys was their youth and hunger. They reminded me of a bunch of pirates. Their team work was a bond formed from having grown up together. They took no prisoners and backed each other all the way, but they were

Life Trails

friendly and open too. Something about this band of brothers really intrigued me. Our club didn't have that 'us against the world' mentality. I wanted in; I wanted that mentality. Over the weeks that passed, I agreed to meet with them and train. My biggest influences were the Fox brothers, Keith and Morgan. Morgan was the older by a few years and a raw talent who never gave up. Keith was similar but probably had to work harder than Morgan in terms of effort. I couldn't help but respect them. They came from a very sporty family and had a code of honesty and fair play imprinted on their DNA. There is something about being around people who are better than you at something that stops you resting on your laurels. Complacency is a killer for any sort of self-improvement. Keith was slightly older than I, and we became regular training partners. We would ride from our houses and meet halfway to talk about school, girls, and training. A new era was dawning and the time for change was coming. Primary school was finished and I was now in secondary school at Ferbane Vocational. More changes, more learning. Graduating *to* high school was mind blowing. Everything I knew was rendered null and void and replaced with a respect for the new world order into which I stepped. Ferbane Vocational School, or the 'Tech' as it was called, was seven km from Cloghan. Most of the kids in the village went to school in Banagher after primary school. I felt left out again because I was part of the minority going to a different town. I

The Second Lap

could never shake the feeling that the division from the other kids in my village was a lifelong stigma. I remember taking a trip to London to see my dad's brother Billy when Susan and I were young. I was eleven years old and our parents had agreed to put us on a plane, solo. Uncle Billy had invited us the year previously, on a visit to Ireland to see us. He was a dapper guy with his hair greased back, not a single strand out of place. He was always freshly shaven and smelled of aftershave, a man who took great pride in his physical appearance. Our trip to the British capital was a major turning point for me, maybe as significant as cycling. My cousins Gary and Darren, Billy and Aunt Liz's sons, were older than us and seriously savvy city kids. The family lived in Kilburn, north London, which was a huge Irish area in the eighties. Our cousins listened to the Beastie Boys—I recall *Licensed to Ill* being on constant rotation. They had earrings and trendy clothes, and I wanted to be like them. Three weeks of visiting all the London sights and seeing different cultures everywhere (I had never seen a black or Indian or Chinese person before, and it was invigorating) had changed me. I did not want to return home. However, home I went knowing something that the rest of my friends didn't, that outside the stifling routine of the life I knew, there was another world that had characters and adventure. Barriers had been broken.

A year later when we revisited London with our parents and little Simon in tow, I convinced my mother to let me get my ear pierced like my cousins.

Life Trails

I came back to school in Cloghan—the beginning of the last primary school year—with an earring, tight jeans and knee-high Doc Martens. I was a regular little punk! If the majority of the kids were going elsewhere then, I, as usual, went the opposite way.

9

Inroads

THE 'TECH' TOOK a while to adjust to. I spent my days quietly observing and trying to suss out who was who. There were the tough guys, there were the geeks, there were the sports guys, and then there were the ladies. My first major crush was on a girl named Tara. If I got busted once for turning around to stare at her, I got busted a thousand times. The teachers were an even mix of male and female. Some inspired you to want to do well and some you just wanted to hit over the head with a chair. I don't remember liking a single class except metal work or geography. Mathematics was pure pain—the numbers made my head hurt. Wood working was bearable, but I was too busy launching timber missiles at the kid in front of me. I struck up an immediate friendship with Jimmy and

Inroads

Derek, two local rebels in my class with an unrivalled ability to answer back in the most sarcastic of ways. The teachers made sure we sat as far apart as was physically possible in order for the class to function. I still had my cycling during the week and also spent the occasional weekend at the Fox household for training and hanging out. (I had left my old club due to differences in approach by the senior guys; it was a wise move and being with Athlone C.C. was rejuvenating in so many ways.) I had started to cycle to school after an agreement I struck with my mother. She would give me the bus money instead to spend on things I needed. My love for music really started to bloom too, and discovering a new band gave you certain credibility. If you had the cassette before the masses, people buzzed around you asking for copies. Having the extra cash meant I could splurge a few pounds now and then on a new tape. On Sunday mornings, one of the national channels, RTE 2, had a music broadcast called the *Beatbox*. It was a TV show hosted by the garrulous Ian Dempsey, who played videos of new artists and trendy bands. This show was bliss. It clashed with the Sunday morning training rides, but Susan would tape it for me. Many new bands were exploding on the scene in the early nineties. Nirvanas' *Nevermind* had just been released, and the lead single *Smells Like Teen Spirit* encapsulated the youth's angst and showed that a long-haired punk rock outsider, like the band's singer Kurt Cobain, could speak for a generation. "Spokesman for Generation X" the magazines called

The Second Lap

him, and it was a tag that probably killed him years later in the form of his own suicide after a long battle with heroin. But from my perspective, it was accurate, nonetheless, because at that age identifying with anything in the world is challenging. Suddenly, being a music-head was cool and being in a band meant you were someone. It wasn't until I came back from a training ride one Sunday and Susan said to me, "Mally, there is this new band called Pearl Jam, you'll love them, loud guitars and long hair," that I realised what I'd been missing.

The following week, she screams from the living room to come in and check their video out. I was still in my cycling gear and dripping sweat, what I saw changed my life forever. *Even Flow* was Pearl Jam's first single from their début album *Ten*. When there is a paradigm shift in the way you view something, it stays with you for the entire journey of life. This was a sound that was new; it wasn't reinventing the wheel, but I could feel it deep down. It wasn't contrived or trying too hard either. It had an energy that lifted the spirit and I just knew that these guys cared about what they did. That was the start of grunge. What I know about the whole movement that spawned in Seattle would take up an entire tome in itself. It became an overnight cultural phenomenon. My passion for this band was instant. I started to trade tapes in school of these buzz bands that sprouted in the wake of Pearl Jam. If one needed a Sonic Youth, Alice In Chains, or Screaming Trees album and so on, I was the go-to-guy. I made mix

Inroads

tapes for my friends with hand designed inlay cards and added every last detail I could get my hands on. Google didn't exist. I pored over dozens of magazine articles, listened to every interview back in the days when MTV was really a music channel and not just a vehicle for bump-and-grind R&B videos like it is today. I became an encyclopedia on these bands, not content with just delivering the music to my friends. I needed to know the musicians and *their* interests, the music *they* listened to and who produced their albums and if they said something about another group, I could recite any number of quotes from memory. Of course not everyone got the movement. The football playing idiots were still posturing, threatening to kick our butts for growing our hair long. They were listening to Garth Brooks and Brian Adams, go figure. The divide for me was a privilege. The friendship between Derek and I grew stronger as we swapped stories about rockers like Hendrix, REM, and Stevie Ray Vaughan to name but a few. My cycling buddy, Keith, was also becoming a fan of grunge and our training-ride chats were based on the subjects of a similar nature to Derek and mine. It meant that we select few had a private membership to something that was still semi-underground. It began to get bigger after a while and one morning in the library before school started, I met my best friend who has been by my side since that day over twenty years ago.

As he lived just on the outskirts of town, Trevor was a local by Ferbane standards. He was in

The Second Lap

my sister Susan's class, a year ahead of me. I had seen him around and had heard about him from Susan—he was cool and everybody liked him. I was a bit dubious in the beginning because he hung out amongst the music guys but also with the footballers and other 'groups' too. Just how cosy he was with the so-called enemy unconsciously led me to tread carefully. Back to the morning in the library—Pearl Jam had just made their TV début in England recording a song on the popular late-night BBC music program, *The Late Show*. This was a cutting-edge show that got the cream of the crop as far as new talent was concerned and they got them down on tape before anyone else. The channel commissioned a night called 'No Nirvana', which was a cheeky wink at the fact that other bands did exist outside the behemoth that the band had become. A guy in Trev's class had recorded it so anyone with an ounce of cool piled into the library to check out the recording. *Alive* was the song that Pearl Jam played, and again, they raised the bar; it's a song that has incredible groove but subtle in places too and ends with a blistering Hendrix-inspired solo. The subject matter deals with the singer, Eddie Vedder's, tragic learning that his father was not his biological dad and that his real father was a family friend who had passed away. In the narrative, he wrestles with the fact that he is cursed and still 'Alive' when he feels like his life has been a lie and he has nothing left to live for. Trev happened to be in the room at the same time and I remember seeing the look on his face after it. We

Inroads

both just stared at each other with expressions of amazement before I approached him.

"It's Trev, right? I'm Malcolm, Susan's brother."

"Hey man, so what do you think? Pearl Jam are incredible, huh?"

Life was becoming more realised, passion had become a new and tangible entity and replaced a lot of the unhealthy obsessions within me. At fifteen I felt open, fulfilled, and I also had a person who loved all the things I did and we could share them openly and without fear of judgement. I began writing journals around this time and felt a release in this private world of mine. Journaling was a form of expression that would give my wandering mind a place to interpret life as I saw it.

10

Unwritten

MATURING IS BIZARRE. Full stop. No one hands out a manual when you enter your teenage years. Peer pressure is the single biggest reason behind all the crazy antics and mistakes that we make going through that passage. Youth is wasted on the young, but that's the way it should be right? I mean if you can't make the mistakes, then you can't really say you've lived, can you? Maybe making the mistakes is the manual and that through them, the future is written. There are so many ways that young men especially can benefit from the right guidance, and then there are the distractions along the route that can result in everything going wrong. Society lacks a way to enhance the lives of teenagers by really failing to teach them self-worth and appreciating who they are, the way

Unwritten

they are. Sure, mocking is part and parcel of being in school, and I've intimidated plenty in my time. That will never go away. The thing that can change, however, is boosting young adults' lives through making them feel unique and important because if you don't, then they only believe the yard chatter. I don't think it's as simple as that all the time, but it is a right place to start. Why do I have this point of view? Because I've been there and had some great adults to guide me through life and support things I did, adults who believed in the inclusion of all regardless of height, weight, or any other so-called socially awkward incompatibility.

The one universal litmus test for young men the world over is, unfortunately, alcohol! Booze is the sure-fire way to prove to everyone that you have the balls to do something and to think you are a tough guy. It was the ancient tribes which took their sons to the mountainside and sat with them as they learned about the outdoors or how to hunt their own food. These rituals formed a sacred bond passed down from generation to generation, a sharing of knowledge and the esteem of being elevated to manhood. Our culture is to get drunk, and in Ireland that's only too easy. I have lived in many places the world over in the past eleven or so years and the first thing I'm asked when my nationality is discovered is, "Fancy a drink?" It is as automatic as asking how I am, a not too inaccurate stereotype of our nation and not something that should instil pride. I had my first drink at a wedding in England when I was

The Second Lap

probably thirteen years old. My cousin Damien and his older friend (who I think was called Chris) had stolen some beers. Chris' dad would never miss them I was told. It was not like I was going to turn around and say no because I did not know what to expect—I saw adults doing it, so I presumed it was fair game for me too. My impression of the taste was pretty typical though, it was bitter and horrible and when I puked my guts up, I swore against it forever. It was a grudge that did not last and down the line, alcohol became so interwoven in the fabric of my life that it almost killed me.

The role of music as art was, in essence, the accelerator for pursuing my writing on a deeper level. On the page, it's impossible to lie. A façade can be put on in front of friends, parents, and teachers, but nothing is more transparent than the reflections of your own mind in print. I should have been devoted to English class, but I couldn't bear the excuse of a teacher we had. Gary was an arrogant and intolerant man who coached the hurling team, and if you could hurl, you got an easy ride. I couldn't play well, hence my mischief-making accounted for many a day spent outside his class waiting for the principal to come and box my ears, as he loved to do. My adolescent brain had hoped moving forward in school would transform the experience from one of pain and suffering to one of mutual respect and nurture. I was wrong. It was the same game, only the players had changed.

Unwritten

English class was like church—if they wanted your opinion, they would give it to you. I had visions and desires to be a journalist. I didn't care what kind of journalist; I just wanted to be paid to write. I didn't want to be a millionaire or a superstar; just to live frugally/modestly in front of a note pad or typewriter in a small cabin somewhere with an endless supply of beer and dream about being the next Charles Bukowski or Hunter S. Thompson. English class, however, was really an education in what not to be as a writer or a person. The more material that went into my private books and journals, the less I was willing to share in the class. I dreamt of a teacher who would take me under his or her wing and nurture the rough diamond I imagined myself to be. I prayed I would find my role in this hell-hole of daily grind. But my suggestion to take the honours class was laughed at in ridicule and disbelief. How can a teacher do this? Isn't their *raison d'être* to mould the young and take them to higher levels, instead of stooping to a bike-shed mentality themselves? I saw ignorance and favouritism in every educational institution I attended, which still baffles me. I fail to see the sense in education being about anything other than that, education. Nevertheless, for every douchebag with a temper or a complex, there were two teachers who made it worthwhile. Mrs. Brodie was our Irish and Geography teacher in our third year. She was mature, confident, and when she walked it was like the Earth's axis rotated on her hips. I wouldn't say her beauty was very obvious

The Second Lap

in the way that if you saw her in a supermarket or walking down the street your jaw would drop. She probably knew she was hot because she had that swagger that just radiated it. She dressed nicely and wore bright cerise pink tights, and just-above-the-knee skirts. A double class with her was not only pleasing to my eyes—she also challenged the class. There was no free ride with her—you did the work or she called you out. She was also less inclined to play the favourite's game with the dumb footballers. The girls hated her because the boys all loved her. The ultimate dilemma in my pubescent mind would have been choosing between her and Tara. The fact that one was a married woman with two kids and the other was a girl in my class that didn't know I existed made it all the funnier. Once a dreamer, always a dreamer. My relationship with Mrs. Brodie was deeper I think than anyone else's. On the days when I couldn't be bothered to ride my bike to school, I would hitch-hike, and on occasion, she would stop to pick me up as she lived on the same stretch but in a town further south. I would sit in her VW and breathe in her perfume and fantasise about me and her in the back seat. It was never a perverted kind of lust after her, because I really liked her deep down. She was everything to me because of her fairness and her drive to get the best out of us. She was one of the first people to call me Mally and any time there was a reference to 'Mali' in Africa, she would crack up and call me "Mally from Mali." The car rides became a thing between us that I loved. The

Unwritten

journey was ten minutes, but I could've stayed in that car with her driving all day. I also appreciated how she would confide in me and with great sadness one morning she did. As she slowed the car for me to jump in, it struck me that she did not look herself, her eyes were red, and she looked exhausted. I asked her if there was anything the matter. Her trembling hands gripping the wheel, she broke down recounting the story of how her husband had been driving back from work just a week earlier when his Mercedes was struck by a wheel that had flown off the truck in front of him. His car took a major hit sending him off the motorway; the crash was pretty bad as was his condition. I pictured a bruised body with tubes sticking out of it and the sound of a breathing apparatus masking her sobs in an otherwise silent hospital room. She leaned over my legs to the glove compartment and pulled out the circular three-pronged metal badge that is the signature on the front of every Mercedes car. When she told me this was pretty much all that was left of his car, I could have cried for her. I wanted to hold her in my arms and stroke her hair and tell her it would be alright. But I was just a teenager. Her husband would pull through after a slow recovery. She did show me, though, that no matter what age you are, it's important to be yourself and retain one's individuality instead of running with the herd. I know that if she had been my English teacher, my professional life may have turned out differently.

The Second Lap

Tim O'Reilly was another teacher who played the game in an antithetic manner—a curly-haired canoeing, mountaineering, and outdoor pursuit's enthusiast from County Cork with a penchant for corduroy pants and throwing smarmy students through the doors of metal lockers. Sure, other teachers threw their weight around too, but with him, you must have deserved it. Metal work and technical drawing were his subjects, and he knew them inside out. There is something fascinatingly enthralling for me about people who know their subjects. The subject itself is just a minor detail; the most important factor is the person's connection to it and love for it. In my eyes it means you care about *something* at least. That passion then has a ripple effect and can in turn influence other people in a positive way.

The waiting area outside of the metal work room was located in the older part of the school building, thus giving it the feeling of being far removed from the vigilance of authority. Bedlam is the first word that comes to mind in describing it. Heads were stuck down toilets, chewing gum pressed into hair, headlocks, and 'scrubs' (having your head polished by the knuckles of someone at least a foot taller than you) were all *de rigueur* at the time. No matter what happened, no one told. It was simple. You took the beating or the hair rinse in the cubicle and then they moved on to someone else. If you snitched you might as well have castrated yourself because it would only be a matter of time before the mob did

Unwritten

it for you. So, knowing that you had less chance of getting caught by the principal and *more* chance of getting caught by O'Reilly, made it too irresistible. It was like Eve in the Garden of Eden or a super massive black hole: you got sucked in.

In order to wait for O'Reilly to come down and open the door, we had to queue outside in single file with our backs to the wall. This made us sitting ducks for the older guys to cherry-pick a ripe piece of flesh and get down to work. One of the most effective methods of torture was subtle but resonated long after the act had happened. A student would lean against the wall to economise on the effort of standing, thus leaving all the weight on his legs. The offender only had to launch a kick at the kid's ankles and their legs shot straight out as their butt took the full weight of the blow on the concrete floor. If, however, O'Reilly caught you involved in any such shenanigans, the full bellow that emanated from those altitude assisted lungs let any living thing within fifty feet know all about it. I had never heard a teacher pulverise dudes for stepping out of line like this, and that was just his voice—he didn't give a hoot who you were. He was the lion king and that was that. I loved him. He was so nature driven and had a tremendous depth of knowledge on the things he liked and the things I found important in life. It was confidence and he had nothing to prove. He was the head of outdoor pursuits adventures for the school and every year took a group of students to a hostel in Birr, about

The Second Lap

thirty km away. For many, it would be the first real trip away from home, a total immersion of activities that were hated by some and loved by others. It felt invigorating to fill the days with abseiling, hiking, canoeing, and orienteering—a chance to be self sufficient and humbled by nature. Being held in the ever flowing caress of a river that carries you along serenely one minute and can turn on you in an instant or being dwarfed on a mountainside by the sheer grandiosity of its mass is what it means to live. It's moments like those where time stands suspended from all the false realities that humans invent to make themselves financially richer, or in their own minds, better than the rest. Land and the living things that inhabit it give human beings so much, but our ignorance and arrogance to imagine we can take it all and give so little back shows how misguided and selfish we can be. I think it was those three days exploring and talking to Tim that made me realise that freedom of the mind out in the wilderness is a meditation of sorts.

It wasn't all sublime revelation though. Put a load of the same guys who kick the crap out of each other in class into one big hostel room and turn out the lights, now there's a party you don't wanna miss. Lights went out, and then a thud and a scream would be heard. Lights would go on again and some boy would be half naked on his mattress in the middle of the floor. Lights go off, and a huge fire ball would appear in the middle of the room. Our pal Fozzy had taken his party piece to a larger audience it seemed.

Unwritten

His thing was to jig the valve on a gas cigarette lighter and turn it up to the maximum. He would then suck the gas into his mouth and blow out a ball of flame that illuminated the hostel room and probably took most of his eyebrows with it. In a time where most kids were afraid of smoking, Fozzy was on a pack a day, and breathing fire was just a natural extension of his habit.

11

Relentless

THIS WAS NOT the only change in my life. My love for music was blooming. I no longer was content being the guy who kept people current through cassettes. I wanted to—I had to—express myself through an instrument. I just didn't know which one. Looking back, I think what you end up playing is preordained. Derek was becoming dexterous and fluid on his guitar and he was pretty much self-taught. He idolised the guys who mattered, Stevie Ray Vaughan, Hendrix, and Pearl Jam's six-string prodigy Mike McCready, whose blistering leads he tried to emulate every time he picked up his own battered guitar. Trev had 'bass player' written all over him, no arguments there. I envisioned myself as the one behind a kit letting it all go—thinking of school bullies' heads whilst bashing the snare drum

Relentless

with all my might. Our friend Neil was coming on board as the second guitar player and would add depth to Derek's wizardry. He also smoked like the Marlboro Man and had a way with some seriously popular and hot girls. Things were taking shape, but I had still not found my niche in the grand scheme of this plan for world domination. At first I thought I'd be the keyboard player, the guys laughed. The 1993 MTV awards was a paradigm shift. Pearl Jam was playing and they played it hard. They had just released their second album and turned their backs, in a way, to the publicity spin that magazines lamely put out in order to shift copies. It may be a big fat paradox that they did this while appearing on the largest music television channel in the world, but they certainly played by their own rules. They crushed it on their new single, *Animal*, but it was when Neil Young joined them for *Rockin' in the Free World*—his gargantuan anthem on social issues in contemporary America—that they cut through the sonic barriers like a scythe. The whole thing was flawless, yet retained a punkiness too. One guy stood out to me as he powered it all with his unique and jazzy flair—drummer Dave Abbruzzese. Seeing him, I was sold hook, line and cymbals. I wanted to be that guy. I wanted to feel what it was like to experience music so tangibly.

The conflict between cycling and my increasing musical passion soon became evident. These two tectonic plates in my life bumped hard against each other, taking my heart in different directions.

The Second Lap

For a time, I could separate the two, but I started to feel as if I had two lives, as if I had to always be the chameleon. I decided what I wanted most was to be a rock drummer—and a writer. Slowly the interest in cycle training waned. Instead I was studying musicians and their movements on videos, dissecting live shows with surgical precision. Not a beat or a hi-hat nuance was missed and my always obsessive and elephantine memory stored it all. I had no idea how to coordinate my two hands and feet independently from each other, but with my video lessons I knew it *could* be done. The next step was to find a kit. Trev's cousin Gaz had been bashing around in a local band that had been the first group to really play anything that qualified as a *gig*. His group had a van and they all had driving licences. I remember walking into one of their rehearsals and being mesmerised by the amount of equipment, amps, guitars, effects pedals, and drums. It looked legit and they could play modern songs from start to finish. Talk about whetting my appetite. It was decided that Gaz was the guy to approach to get this up and running. He *very* hastily agreed to lend us his kit providing it was well taken care of. But there was one issue—getting the kit from Gaz's to St. Mary's Hall, which was going to be our future practice spot. None of us drove and it was a bit of a haul on foot. Who would be willing to lend a hand to a bunch of hairy youths with stars in their eyes? Tim O'Reilly enthusiastically offered his canoe laden van. He appreciated what we were doing, going

Relentless

against the grain and expressing ourselves through music instead of following the herd into sport. The drive was only five minutes but I thought we would never get there, I rode up front with Tim, and Derek crouched in the back seats peering out between us. Turning into the driveway, I jumped out of the still moving van and ran over to lift the sliding metal garage door. It was dark inside but the drums' black gloss finish was contrasted by gleaming silver fittings that shone like cats' eyes in the night. I was instantly drawn into a love affair. It felt dangerous, seminal, forbidden. Arriving at the hall, my first hurdle was how to set up the drums. Of course, I had put no forethought into this at all. The constant dreaming of powering a band along with my groove took precedent over anything practical like how to assemble my instrument, which wasn't as simple as plugging a lead into an amp! I was flustered with cymbal stands, clumsily adjusting the heights of toms, and feeling embarrassed as my friends watched it all. I raised the seat too high, had my snare drum too low, cymbal stands that weren't tightened would move every time I hit one, my arms ached after five minutes due to my inability to loosen up.

Finally, after bluffing my way to a set up that I felt looked semi-professional (looks were everything) and feeling I could get away with a basic beat, we were ready. Derek officially kicked us off with the chords to *Rockin' in the Free World*. This was what the moment had condensed to, me and my two sticks waiting to power in and set the train rolling.

The Second Lap

I hesitated slightly at first but channelled everything I had seen and heard in the past few weeks of video study time. My timing was a little rough to start, but we had music in the air and it was being made by *us*.

12

Mic Check

PLAYING MUSIC AND playing it well as a group is all about chemistry and feel. Technical proficiency means nothing unless the shared ethic amongst all the musicians is about being totally selfless to the songs. Bands that work have a respect for the craft. The ones populated with egos usually implode. To say that "becoming more popular because we were a band" didn't interest us would be a lie. We all felt a connection beyond being close friends. This was an evolution of our friendship. With time, we had improved. Occasionally we would have a breakthrough on a tough piece of music; Trev would nail a funky and complex Chili Pepper's bass line or Derek would lay down a note for note perfect rendition of the classic Hendrix song, *Little Wing*. We were finding

The Second Lap

our way. We did it together and grew alongside each other. I would feel great satisfaction when the guys challenged me with some sort of polyrhythmic beat and I was capable of mastering it. With rehearsals executed, what we really needed was a gig to test ourselves against other groups. There wasn't much of a local scene around Ferbane, just some usual suspects who either couldn't play well but thought they could or those who could and just didn't seem bothered. I wasn't interested in being stuck in the hall forever or in my bedroom air-drumming to CD's. I wanted to know what it felt like to be in front of an audience. That required one more member. My old friend Poochie from school days came on board as a singer, and we were ready to start playing some pub gigs. But before we could move in any direction, we needed a name. One day in between classes, Derek and I were scribbling random words on our note pads with the intention of coming up with a memorable treble-barrelled name. Somehow the word 'tear' (as in tear something apart, not the tear from an eye—for years after, the misinterpretation of this drove us up the walls) started the future of our name. I remember thinking of 'Lane' and 'Hash' after that. I liked that it had a lane in the name, like a path that we walked down together. The hash was thrown in to make it sound stoned and druggie and cool. The actual substance was also starting to be smoked by many of our fellow students, so that added value to the name too. We were *Tear Lane Hash*. If we became the greatest band in the world,

Mic Check

it would have been an equally great name, but when you are a struggling five-piece that will remain forever unknown outside the county of Offaly, well, it's just hard to pronounce and even harder to spell. But what's in a name, right? Tear Lane Hash was officially born in the local pubs playing covers for minimal pay that kept younger drinkers shelling out the money they robbed from their parents. We had arguments regularly over song choices and how much of our so-called integrity we were willing to give up by playing radio hits. Reflecting now, it's funny, but back then personalities were strong and it was a healthy kind of sparring. We wanted to be taken seriously and we drilled ourselves to get the tunes dialed in. The Ball O'Malt pub was where we honed our skills and pushed each other to pull off something that we or other bands hadn't done before. It was a smoky, rectangular-shaped place with dark reddish-brown carpet, old-fashioned wall paper, and dodgy lamp fittings protruding from the walls. The long wooden bar that stood to the right of the entrance was a no-frills affair with a brass rail and overflowing ashtrays atop its pockmarked surface. On the weekends, it was three deep with acne-covered youths craning their necks and waving cash in the hope of getting a pint. It didn't have many windows, two at the front that we only saw when we entered and left. The music action was at the rear, and the low ceilings gave it a basement feel. The band's place was underneath the television set just beside the door to the bathrooms. Any time a

The Second Lap

friend went to take a leak, they'd give us the thumbs up and if we were lucky, pass us a beer. We were not reinventing the wheel, but we wanted to put our stamp on the place. At the time, most pub bands were nothing more than a few older guys with a drum machine who churned out the standard boring songs to keep feet tapping and pint glasses raised. Being a pipe and slippers band just didn't cut it for us. In order to keep it fresh, we peppered the sets with classics and some twists on more well-known numbers. Our apprenticeship served, it was time to start entering Battle of the Bands contests.

The feelings we had about our music echoed the sentiments of kids across the country as Battle of the Bands shows started to pop up everywhere. We were incredibly lucky that all our parents were supportive of everything we did. Neil had left the band at this stage. We needed a solid replacement, and our friend Brian came on board. He played well and was a really good guy; we ribbed him endlessly for his love of Bon Jovi and big hair rock and when we gave him the nickname Chesney Hawkes, there was no going back. We gave him grief because we cared. For the shows, our families took turns in being our 'crew' on different weekends. It was so much fun being on the road and turning up at various nightclubs to play for people. Real rock n' roll! We had to up our game considerably to be heard above the more experienced groups. Having been in our own little local bubble we thought we were the bee's knees. In bigger towns, like Moate or

Mic Check

Tullamore, we were just another bunch of wannabes. But we weren't intimidated. I think because of the friendship, we had an 'us against them' mentality, much like a gang. Just because you looked like a rock star with an expensive guitar or a bandanna on your head, didn't mean you frightened us. We were the underdogs and we fought for scraps too. The first few contests were abysmal. We always ended up being on early when the sound mix was poor. Too often all the equipment was set at a level that couldn't be touched because some sound engineer with a god complex had spent hours setting it all up. One of our greatest nights came on the back of a strange week. I had entered us into the Battle of the Bands at a really prestigious contest in Tullamore, the capital of Offaly. Tullamore was the closest thing for us to Seattle back then—a Petri dish for bands. There was some serious talent and some young groups that could bash out grunge-era songs with an uncanny similarity to the originals. My girlfriend at the time, Serena, lived in the town, and by spending weekends there I befriended a lot of the local guys. I loved drinking beer and talking about various groups and geeking out over drum kits and rock magazines. There was a real camaraderie on the scene and it was where I met Conor and Dermot with whom I would start another group and expand my family tree of bands. The local groups took it upon themselves to organise their own shows and in turn created a whole scene that was really inclusive. It was inspiring to see them all pull together to make

The Second Lap

an event happen. On our run up to the big contest, posters were put up around town with our name on it. Tear Lane Hash was right there beside some of the groups which were considered as big players and guys we hoped we could emulate in popularity. I was very proud, as my role in the band went beyond being just a drummer. I was kind of the manager/PR guy who dealt with getting us into these events. I knew the right people to deal with and knew what would work for us and what wouldn't. Derek would play anywhere, but after all the pub gigs I wanted us to be more selective and had a certain trajectory in mind. This was the starting point of the ascent to the next level, all we had to do was make it there, easy! Having Poochie in the band meant there was never a dull moment.

Poochie was a friend of mine from primary school and was a star from birth. Even as a youngster he would preen for the school photo like a peacock. I swear, that sideways head tilt he did in third or fourth class never changed even in his late teens. He lived outside of Cloghan in the sticks, and he didn't give a dang about anything. Some people are just rock stars, not in the sense that they play to sold-out stadiums every night but in aura and attitude. He just had a *je ne sais quoi* that made you want to be around him and have him on your side. His joining the band was a fluke because we never imagined him to have the voice he had. It was only after he stumbled in, hungover from some girl's place he was sleeping with at the time, that we

Mic Check

found he could wail. He had arrived at the hall on a Sunday morning looking for somewhere to rest his weary mind and body. As we belted out songs, he had decided to wrap himself in some stage curtains and doze off. After he got some shut-eye during all the racket, he resurrected and declared himself sober and reborn. Derek pushed him to try to sing and when he opened his mouth we were stunned; he looked good but he sounded sensational. A star had shot through the night sky and landed in our band. The question was, how long would it take the star to burn out?

Although Poochie's reliability for practice had always been random at the best of times, he never missed a gig, but Poochie struggled with pressure. If the event was a biggie, he crumbled. It was as if he felt he wasn't worthy even though he blew most of the others away on raw talent alone. Still, everything seemed on course for the big Battle of the Bands. I spent the week on the phone to people in the loop making sure it was all covered in a promotional sense and even did an interview with a reasonably decent newspaper telling them about our group. Word was starting to spread that this was going to be a big night, and the other bands on the bill were all killer and no filler. Our 'fans' took it on themselves to hire a minibus and make the twenty-five km journey to the venue, a beautiful hotel called the Bridge House. I couldn't believe that it was happening, but the momentum was right, and I believed our time had come. On the day of the show, I spent most of

The Second Lap

it with friends going over a few last-minute details and listening to songs and feeling really relaxed. The other guys were off doing their own thing, and Poochie was out with our friend Barry in Barry's new car. With everything set by late afternoon and people all ready for a big night out, word filtered through that Barry and Poochie had been in a car accident. Apparently, they had been on the really narrow bog road that connects Cloghan to Ferbane and Barry, being new to driving, was probably being a bit cautious and was maybe too close to the verge. Poochie, feeling nervous and in danger, grabbed the steering wheel from Barry's hands and in the ensuing commotion, the car sailed over a dyke at the side of the road and landed in the bog. The boys were OK but well shaken up and the phone call we received told us that Poochie wasn't sure he'd make it that evening. We were saddened, although really happy that they both came out unscathed, but thought it typical of our luck that this spanner would land in the works. We chose to press on ahead anyway and told him to try his hardest to make an appearance. If not, we would just wing it with Derek filling in on vocals. When we got to the Bridge House, it was surreal—a huge ballroom with balconies and upper-level seating overlooked our stage down below. The lighting in the ball room was a soft red and the mirrorball above the middle of the oval dance floor gleamed like our smiles. This was a big production and the talent was blazin'. I met Serena and some of the other bands from Tullamore that I had gotten

Mic Check

to know well who were playing too. We introduced ourselves to some new groups, who were down to earth but one, whose name eludes me, really stood out. They were a three piece which had gotten some coverage in a newspaper with a photo alongside it. I mean they landed in the ballroom as if they had just gotten off a private jet from Vegas. Sleeveless denim jackets, hair coiffured to perfection (with an ozone destroying amount of hairspray probably), and an air of such laughable extravagance that our eyes just rolled. The running order of the night showed that we were the penultimate band—this was a victory before we even hit a note. We were, without fail, always first on previous occasions. The sound levels would be better and the crowd would be warmed up. Our families all came to support us and our mob was huge, along with the minibus crew we packed it out. It was a huge celebration of having made it there and it was as much about the friendships as about the music. Our buddies from our respective schools had made the effort to come, that was not lost on us; we carried their hopes on our shoulders and when we played we did it for them as well as our parents, too, who had spent so much time and money on making sure we got where we needed to go every weekend. They had driven us home from nightclubs after playing to a handful of people for no recognition and roadied gear without ever questioning our motivations. It made me realise right there and then the music is not about self-aggrandisement or popularity, it's about sharing

The Second Lap

the experience, the moment, and the joy that comes with it. As proceedings were about to get under way Poochie walks in the door, it was like an apparition. No one could believe the events of the day and as he recounted the accident, he showed us the raw seat-belt marks on his neck and the fresh bruising on his wrists and arms. He had come through like a fighter and said he didn't want to let anyone down. Game on. We had gone from shaky ground to rock solid attitude and an unwavering conviction to go out and slay the crowd.

The first few bands were really good and when the posers got up and played a cover song of a then unknown Irish band called My Little Funhouse and claimed as their own, I was furious. Not many people had even heard of this band, but my knowledge was not that of your average music fan, so I called them out on it immediately. The guitarist squared up to me, but I wouldn't back down; cheating was not what our community was about. We were band number seven and when dropped into the groove of Pearl Jam's *Even Flow*, all our crew were jumping the barriers beside the dance floor and swarming the previously vacant space. We were high from adrenaline and joy at seeing people lose themselves with abandon to music that we were playing. I could scarcely make the connection back to the shy and awkward band we were on that first day of rehearsal. We were now a self-assured unit that had worked hard and paid our dues. Tear Lane Hash had arrived. Ending our three song set with our stomping *Rockin'*

Mic Check

in the Free World brought a frenzy to the room. The stage was shaking as we wrought everything from our instruments and ourselves. Poochie's battered body emitting a guttural howl from deep inside, his wounded state refusing to give anything less than his all. The symbiosis of moments like that strip away self-importance and replace it with a quiet humility. Being one's own biggest critic, as I've always been, means that you don't have to prove anything to anyone except yourself. That was one of those nights where even though much back slapping and praise from our friends ensued, it was a quiet and unspoken nod amongst the five of us that spoke the loudest. In the end, we came in third place behind two bands, one of which deserved to make it to the final and one of which had some inside pull. That didn't matter to us, I knew that we had played the best we could, and I was proud of how it had all come together. It was not about getting to a final and winning a big prize; it was about contributing to the scene and inspiring the other friends we had that it is possible to pick up and start from scratch, whether it's an instrument or another form of expression. Things would change after that night and yes there would be other memorable performances and nights to recall, but this one had the exultant joy of being in the right place at the right time and everything aligning in an inexplicable way.

13

Formation

THE FINAL EXAM, the leaving certificate, was looming on the horizon. For me, it would be good riddance to the school. We would of course rock our graduation night with a three song set, and I would witness Poochie making off with my date for the night. But I didn't care. I had no real plans for after school because I truly didn't know what I wanted to achieve with my life. Who does at that age? I know some people had a vague idea, but I was lost. I was enjoying making music and couldn't see far enough down the line to commit to a career of any sort. College was never mentioned in our house, so I would just take my chances. I enrolled in an F.A.S. course (an Irish job training organisation that offered various courses from electrical work to mechanical engineering and

Formation

computers). The class titled "Engineering," turned out to be a glorified term for welding stuff together and trying to stay out of trouble. It was held in a community workshop in Athlone. On my first day there I met some of the sneakiest and dodgiest people I have ever encountered. That said, many of them were pretty funny. Most had grown up on the wrong side of the tracks and never gotten their leaving certificates. Their education was the school of hard knocks. There wasn't a minute where they weren't trying to shaft each other. The language was foul and if you looked at one of them crooked, there was a good chance you would have the living daylights hammered out of you with a steel rod.

Two days into the course during a welding assessment, a kid named Oggy lifted my protective mask blinding me with the glare. I spent the next two nights unable to sleep—my eyes felt scorched, as if they were packed with sand. Had there been a course in engineering ways to be as ruthless and crude as humanly possible, these guys would be top scholars. Still, once I got to know them I realised their actions were born out of their rough early lives, whereas I had all the support in the world from my own parents with cycling and music, some of these guys rarely went home. Some stole money whenever they needed from wherever they could. And they smoked a lot of hash. Using substances to alter your brain chemistry was something I could already relate to—and here was a new one.

The Second Lap

I loved to drink beer. The year before, as Trev was older than me, he had gotten a job as a grease monkey at a garage in Tullamore. It paid him forty pounds a week and that became drinking money for us. The ritual was simple: the local off-licence in Ferbane, Hineys, had a deal: five pounds for six cans of Tennent's. The stuff was poison, but it was cheap and it contained alcohol. Job done. Every Friday Trev would finish work, go home and shower off the grease and oil he spent the day wading through, and then make tracks to my house with the twelve beers. I don't think my mother was too impressed, but she never vociferously protested. Friday was also a bonus because it was *The Word* on Channel 4 and chances were that if something was breaking in the world of music, that's where you would see it first. It was an orgy of rock, alcohol, debauchery, movie stars, swearing, and controversy. We loved it because by the time it hit the screen after eleven o'clock, we were as inebriated as the guests themselves. Trev and I were tight—we played in a band together, drank together, and laughed hard together. When you have a friend like that, you think everything in the world is going to be OK. Our parents had also known each other for years. They probably thought we were a bit mad, but I sensed they trusted us.

When you get as accustomed to drinking as I had, you then tend to be curious about other substances too. Until the F.A.S. welding class, hash was a box I hadn't ticked yet. For the guys in class, it was easy to get. One Friday, after we received our

Formation

pay for what was basically raising hell, Oggy asked who was in. I decided that I'd get some and see how it went down. The first time was a bit of a wash out. My memory is vague, but it involved me turning white and there may have been some vomit. No sources can confirm or deny this, so I'll go with my shoddy memory and say it was messy. I would, however, not be denied based on my first experience, and it soon became a regular occurrence. Not a morning ritual of waking up and putting a joint in my mouth, but if it was offered outside a pub, I'd happily participate. We would go for a few drinks occasionally on Fridays too and all have a smoke. For me, it was still in that experimental stage. I got a major boost and change in direction after a month in the engineering class when the manager, Frank, called me into his office. A decision had been made to open a new course on desk-top publishing. He asked if I was interested. His opinion was that I was too smart to be in the engineering/hell-raising class and intimated that it was a waste of my time. I can't say I disagreed even though I felt a certain affection for my comrades in welding. I told him I'd be happy to change classes and try something more in line with my interests. I had never been really good with my hands and a subject with a more creative slant seemed a good place to restart. There were seven of us and even though our abilities varied, we were a well-chosen group. Our instructor, Eileen, was laid back and treated us like grown-ups. We learned the basic skills of layout, design, and visual presentation. As

The Second Lap

the class began to meld, some of us started hanging out together outside of the centre. This meant going to pubs right after class or meeting for a drink in the evenings and taking part in pub trivia quizzes. I was the general knowledge and music guy but knew nothing about sport. Two guys did, though, and we also had our socially awkward classmate, David, a veritable talking atlas. He could tell you the mountain ranges in the most obscure corners of the globe. Our complimentary knowledge bases made for a winning trivia team and I felt I had found a real place for myself after the month of rude jokes, flying sparks, and solder. I had hit a groove; I had found a niche in desktop publishing.

On the quiet, I founded a little sideline business. My friend Don in Tullamore had been complaining to me at gigs about how hard it was to get into clubs being under-age. Having gone through it in my mid-teens, I knew the loneliness and pain of exclusion. Now that I was all of seventeen it was a little easier. My idea was simple and made possible with the equipment now at my disposal. I was going to make fake ID's and sell them. I didn't see it so much as a business venture, but rather as an exercise in liberating my fellow brothers-in-arms, freeing them to roam night-spots, hunting for girls and booze. Had I treated it like a business, it might well have lasted until I was busted by the cops.

To make it happen required the right shade of paper that the Garda (Irish police) used to make the ID cards. Easy enough. At the local stationery shop, I

Formation

found a shade of green that matched the official card in both colour and weight. Step two was designing a logo that on cursory inspection would pass for the Garda emblem. I waited for a time when I knew Eileen would be out of the class for half an hour. Then, my crack team and I got down to replicating the design. Once I was satisfied that it would stand up to scrutiny, I began moving all the details on the card into position until it matched the real card Don had given me to copy. The buyers then had to glue on the passport picture and laminate it themselves; I wasn't going to be dealing with photos or people. I would then sell the basic cards to Don. After that, he was on his own. If he or anyone else got caught, that was their problem. I was a phantom that didn't exist. I made the cards on Fridays and took them to Tullamore on Saturdays to hand over to Don at a fast-food restaurant where he gave me the money. I sold them for £5 each. All told, I probably made no more than £125 in my career as a forger. To keep on was too much hassle: I had to get the paper, sneak around to print the cards, and I really didn't fancy getting caught. Doing something *that* illegal long-term held no appeal. I was happy to break the laws that gave me more personal satisfaction: smoking pot and under-age drinking.

And even then, I felt a moral dilemma about putting fake ID's into the hands of kids who were using them to get wasted. After the last batch, I told Don I was out. He asked me not to quit as there was good business to be done, but my mind was made up.

The Second Lap

There was also something more important. I made the decision as a budding drummer that it was time to get my own kit. Gaz's had been very useful, and I'll always be grateful for the help he gave us and always sorry too because the kit he got back was not the kit he lent us, having been through several bands who didn't respect it. I found a music shop in Athlone that allowed weekly payments and was run by a supportive guy named Charlie. He gave a lot to the music community and was a genuine guy with sound advice on instruments. I decided on a Hohner kit that was gloss-white and sounded great. After adding some mid-range cymbals and sticks, I was ready to rock.

Our band's first practice together with it was a big deal. The other boys had been acquiring amplifiers and guitars. Now we were a proper outfit. Charlie took £25 a week from me, and I was always prompt with my payments. He believed me and trusted me and to miss a week would feel like letting him down. Over the next few years we did a lot of business with him and I became very fond of how he operated. He was all about the music and never pushed you into something for profit.

Meanwhile, at the training centre, I was enjoying becoming more adept at desktop publishing, but all the staring at computer screens had started to affect my eyes. I squinted and got headaches regularly until they became so troublesome that I made an appointment with an ophthalmologist in Dublin.

Serena and I made a day trip. After the examination the ophthalmologist told me I did indeed need

Formation

specs for computer work and reading. I was a bit bummed but also excited as glasses would change my face a little. Like many guys my age, I didn't like the way I looked that much. Any change was a good change, especially one that made me look smarter. I ended up picking these huge, round, granny glass frames. To me at the time, however, they were *haute couture*. Wearing them did make it a lot easier to read and I welcomed the reprieve from the headaches.

I drummed a lot during the week and every weekend we got together to work out new music. I'd occasionally stay a Friday night in Athlone to hang with the Fox family and the rest of the club. We were all drinkers now and even though they trained hard, we would get wasted. I'd then hitchhike back to Ferbane on a Saturday morning to jam for the weekend. Such great times in hindsight, unencumbered by the worries that parents have: mortgages, kids, jobs, and buying clothes and groceries. I lived out of a backpack and was likely to end up on a friend's couch or floor on any given day of the week. If my parents saw me at all on the weekends it was because I was coming back to change clothes, pick up CD's, or just eat a hearty meal before getting back on the road. I hitch-hiked everywhere and I loved it. There were many times when I got stuck at a crossroads in the middle of nowhere late at night and stood under a lone street light as bats swooped overhead. The transience of the road and the people I met made it gratifying. There is an inner need for us all to tell our story to

The Second Lap

someone else, and that is always simpler to do in the company of a stranger. I heard tales of the most heart-wrenching sadness from older people whose husbands or wives had died leaving them alone after a half a century together. I heard stories from people who had done something terrible in life and used me as their confessional. I heard the tales of crazy people, sad people, happy people, generous people, and perverted people. They all became a part of my life on the road. The most interesting rides would be when I'd hop in and the guy would ask, "Can you skin up?"—a reference to rolling a joint. I'd reply "Sure," and he would proceed to pull a lump of hash out of his shirt pocket. I'd get busy with it. Stoned conversations about the most random of topics passing between strangers whilst rolling through the green countryside was a fun pastime. Sometimes I would be so high I'd have to ask my pilot to drop me off a mile or so before my house so I could walk the rest of the way to straighten myself out before looking my parents in the eye. I always feared I'd start giggling as soon as I looked at them. Drinking and smoking pot for me was not an escape yet, that would come later in life: it was about enhancement and exploration of my mind. I was able to tap into a different part of myself under the influence of these drugs and that excited me. I believed that there were a fundamental truth and purpose in life and that by experimenting in different states of being, it was possible to ask bigger and bolder questions.

Formation

As it turned out, LSD was the ultimate destination on my quest for mind expansion. My only question back then was, where could I buy a ticket?

****

The plane jarred as the wheels let down on the tarmac. I could barely process that the flight was over, I had been so engrossed in my childhood review.

Ha! Where to find LSD? What an idiot I was back then. I still wasn't getting that I had not only 'bought' the ticket, I was boarding the descent into madness. These next few years in London were going to make those beginning years in Ireland, when I thought I was so tough and invincible—and deserving, seem like child's play before I would realise that I was out of control and unable to stop on my own.

Invincible! That's my new theme, I boasted to myself, *Look out London, here I come.* I could hardly wait to hook up with my pals. And, as I hopped on the train, I mumbled under my breath, "Bring it on!"

14

The Ledge

STEPPING INTO LONDON life is like hitting the fast forward switch, akin to walking on an airport travelator as the pace picks up. If you don't pick up your pace, you're left behind. After a quick shuttle from the airport, Trev was waiting at Victoria station for me. Our grins said it all; we were now on an adventure *together*. He had spent some time in mainland Europe working after I'd returned to Ireland from Australia, and it was only now we were synchronising. After having slept on each other's floors and sofas for many years, sharing a house seemed like a dream come true. The excitement of seeing our pad called for celebrations before we even arrived there. Trev took me to his place of employment. It was a modern place called Bar 38 that catered to business folks

The Ledge

who populated busy Hammersmith in West London. I was impressed. He introduced me to his friends and his boss, Frenchie, a feisty blond with a cheeky smile; she gave us a round on the house to welcome me. After catching up over beer and three shots of whatever was handed to me, we eventually made the twenty-minute bus ride to our first-floor apartment in Chiswick. There was a fried chicken takeaway and a general store just below. First stop, naturally, was the store for a bottle of Jack Daniels, bottle of coke, and a bag of ice. Trev had some weed in his room so we were set.

My first impressions were very positive. It was a reasonably-sized, three-bedroom place split over two levels. Trev and his girlfriend shared the only room on the lower floor which was sandwiched in between the living room and the bathroom. Adjoining the bathroom was the kitchen; it was small and square with a cheap-looking off-tan coloured table in the middle, double fridge in the corner, and a surprisingly clean-looking white cooker. Upstairs consisted of two rooms with two Polish girls named Kaisa and Anna sharing the larger one, the third room, mine, was beside theirs. It was clean and airy and caught the sunlight perfectly; it was sparsely furnished with an ornate iron double bed and a cheap Ikea wardrobe; a writing table sat in the corner opposite the window. Being at the rear of the building meant no traffic noise to keep me awake at night. I would later discover that traffic noise was going to be the least of my concerns.

The Second Lap

We all piled into the living room after I briefly unpacked and introductions were made. I knew Trev's girl, Polly, really well, and as it turned out Kaisa was similar to her. She liked drinking, smoking, and partying. A lot. Anna was a square peg trying to fit into a round hole. She was quiet and her disinterest in our way of life was obvious. Smoke soon filled the room and the sound of laughter and clinking whisky glasses kicked off our first night in style. Anna made for the kitchen where she scrubbed the table and the cooker. Now I was starting to see why it looked so presentable. I couldn't see how foreign our lifestyle seemed to her and it must have made her anxious to feel so left out. We had plans to head back out into the city, but the weed really got the better of us. Around four A.M, completely wasted and hoping to beat the sun before it rose, I made it to my bed for my first night in London after a long day. I had no immediate plans for the future. London was my oyster.

My routine soon established itself around Trev's work schedule. He worked a lot of evening shifts at Bar 38, which was very convenient for two night-owls. We would take the bus in together, he'd go to work, and I would prop myself at the bar. Trev poured drinks and flirted with women. I perched at the end of the bar with my journal in front of me. I had left my old journals back in Ireland. I wanted to start afresh, on new pages for a new life. I watched people closely, the masculine guys, flirtatious women, everyone with a story to tell. I wrote

The Ledge

it all down with my black felt-tip pen, sipping on the pints of Guinness Trev put in front of me every half an hour. I mused over where my life would go from here and tried to commit to paper the stream of thoughts whizzing around my head.

The running joke in London was that it was nigh on impossible to meet an English bartender. A mix of Polish, Mexican, Spanish, South African, and Australians appeared to make up the majority of bar workers and waiting staff. I wrote and drank Guinness as strangers patted me on the back asking if I was Trev's friend, Mally. I soon became known as the writer. It made me feel comfortable, like I had found the place where I was supposed to be. Each night after they closed up, the crew would sit down for a few beers. I was a de-facto member of staff. When Trev wasn't working we took trips to the city or hung out at Chiswick Park or Turnham Green getting stoned. His job required tough hours, going to work hung-over almost a requirement. Slinging drinks isn't heart surgery. To his credit, he liked the job, and it suited his affable personality. He made cocktails with pride and, more importantly, always remembered to make enough overspill for us to suck down without a manager noticing.

I had been in London a week and on Saturdays, Bar 38 hosted a vodka and Red Bull promotion—a pitcher of rocket fuel, ridiculously cheap. Frenchie needed fliers handed out on the street and asked me if I would turn on the heat to get more punters in. If I did, it meant free vodka. How could I refuse?

The Second Lap

I cajoled, hustled, and talked every single person I could into the bar and returned an hour later, not a flier in hand.

The place was heaving. You couldn't fit in the door, and the crew struggled to get pitchers washed fast enough. Red Bull stock from the cellar was being carried up five cases at a time and the demand still could not be met. The solution? Frenchie asked me to help out. Soon I was carrying up stock, emptying bins, and collecting glasses from tables. I felt useful and the energy was pumping. The team worked hard and fast, each one depending on the other. After our beers that night, Frenchie offered me a job. I made sure to OK it with Trev as this was his patch and I didn't want to waltz in and step on any toes. He was fine with it. That settled, we raised more glasses and toasted my official start date, Monday. My career in the industry had begun as a *bar back*.

The job of a bar back is the crappiest, most unrewarding job next to dish-washing. The title should be renamed 'dog's body'. It consisted of mopping spillages, collecting and washing glasses so the bartenders had enough cool ones in supply, getting cellar stock and changing beer kegs, fetching ice, and sweeping and checking toilets. If bartenders needed anything, "Mally" was shouted and an order given to get what they needed. It ranged from cranberry juice to cases of red wine and chopping lemons. I wasn't complaining. I was happy to have drinking money and not depend on my savings to pay the rent. I was now in the system.

The Ledge

Navigating London came easy since I lived with people who were in the know regarding the Tube (metro) lines, which buses to take, the most economical ways of moving about the city, and good places to hang out. The variety of our work rotations rarely gave us all time off together and I never knew who would be on the sofa after getting back from a long night at the bar. Sometimes it was quiet and other times a bottle of wine or gin would be on the table, a bunch of new faces crowding around it. Anna was never seen apart from daylight hours and she probably suffered the most with her room being right above the noise. No one was bothered when random strangers popped their heads around the door. We were young, and we were living it up.

After getting into the groove with work I found time to write. Sitting at my desk in my little nest and usually aided by a bottle of red wine and a joint, I would spend a minimum of an hour getting some thoughts down. I thought I was on the cusp of genius most of the time: the false confidence of mind-altering substances. The more I indulged the worse my handwriting became and the less sense my thoughts made. I would read back over the material the next day in amusement, my scrawl looking like I'd given a spider LSD, dipped him in ink and let him loose on the page. All the great alcoholic writers I revered had done it effortlessly and made the page come alive, hadn't they? What was wrong with me? Wasn't I drinking enough? In life, everyone

The Second Lap

is searching for something, an identity, a sense of belonging and self-worth. More than anything, I wanted writing to be my identity. I would have to pay my dues—which for now meant the tedious bar back work.

The boredom of my job was shattered like a rock through a car windshield when Trev's friend Rory came to stay with us. Rory was known to everyone and was a lunatic in his hey-day. Stories of his inability to feel physical pain were beyond comprehension to those who heard them. Had I not witnessed the night where Trev stubbed a cigarette out on his *forehead*, after Rory had begged him to, I would have probably thought them ludicrous. Rory himself told another story, this one perhaps urban myth, about his time as a dairy farmer. He was having trouble getting one cow into a stall so he could attach the suction cup to extract the milk. It lit Rory's short fuse, so he dealt with it the only way he knew how, with his fists. He punched the cow square on in the face and dragged her into place.

Did I mention that Rory was a boxer? He thought that a good night out entailed getting the living daylights pummelled out of him. Whether it was in a boxing ring or the car park of a pub was irrelevant. If it involved pain, it didn't really matter. A fight was a fight. Occasionally, Rory would leave the green fields around Ferbane, where he lived for a time, and make a biannual trip to the Big Smoke. Each time resulted in the breakage of a bone, a window, or a door. Not knowing the carnage he would leave

The Ledge

behind was what gave his life a sense of anticipation and excitement. For him, and for others.

"I wonder what he'll do this time, Trev."

"God only knows Mally, God only knows."

Trev knew Rory well and could take care of him. I was a little intimidated because he hated me. We went to separate schools and he was a few years ahead, but he and Trev grew up just across the road from each other. I was a "pussy who read books and thinks he's all smart" and didn't get in as many fights as befitting a warrior like him. But over time he grew to like me by default. Trev and I were a duo—you got one with the other. The first night Rory was in town, Trev took the night off. I was working. Whilst out on the town Trev ended up losing him and returned to the flat alone.

The next morning, a Saturday, Rory turned up looking as dishevelled as a person could be and still be able to stand. He explained how he lost his bearings and found a bunch of Jamaicans who took him around the block in their car smoking large joints. Rory was not a big smoker and the stuff he inhaled just wiped him out. He had wandered the streets for hours before a chance sighting of the corner general store told him his homing beacon was working. He crashed on the sofa immediately.

Later that day Trev and I headed in for the night shift. So far, so good! When Rory walked into Bar 38 a few hours later it was like an apparition. Any other individual would have withered under such extreme intoxication, but not Rory. Not yet. He was a legend

The Second Lap

from the Midlands of Ireland and still on a mission. He started on Drambuie, a sweet, golden-coloured 80 proof liqueur made from malt whisky, honey, and herbs, most commonly used for stripping paint off walls, or in Rory's case, for drinking like water. One of the bartenders, Sam, decided it was not enough to give him single shots, so when Rory motioned for another, Sam hit him with a *treble* shot. After four glasses being thrown down Rory's gullet in what was surely a contender for the Guinness World Record Book's fastest time, he began to wobble. He looked worse than he did after his session with the Rastas, if that was even possible. Trev rounded the bar and told him to head down to a local kebab shop and soak up the liqueur. Rory agreed to satisfy his appetite, and us, by leaving. Sam had been a douchebag by serving him those shots, but we were also complicit in letting it happen.

An hour passed before Rory returned, a true heavyweight if ever I had seen one, back on his feet after a ten count. Now he was drinking beer, slurring badly with his eyes closing. Two sips of his pint and he threw up the entire kebab on the floor of the bar. It was so undigested I could swear that the pita bread came out first before he filled the rest of it with bits of lamb, onions, and salad. The bouncer came over and laid a hand on Rory's shoulder, which was like placing a red cape on a bull. Rory told him to remove his hand, which he did. He then proceeded to drain the rest of his glass and put it on the table. Before he was thrown out, he turned to us at the bar and

The Ledge

muttered, "Rory never leaves a pint behind." Great drama all round but who had to mop up his supper? The bar back. *Moi*. That night I told Frenchie I needed a promotion.

15

Rapture

AFTER HANGING UP my mop and brush, I graduated to pulling beers and concocting cocktails. This was more like it, close contact with pretty girls looking to get drunk. My first weekend shift was a marathon one. On Saturdays, a local club called Hammersmith Palais staged a school disco night where everyone kitted out in school uniforms. It was a fantasy land for those who wanted to live out their desire to get their rocks off whilst dressed as a school kid. I found it to be a mask that brought out what lay below the surface. The same business nine to fivers who dined politely and tipped well during the week turned into moronic, abusive tossers when the costumes came on. Women were debased by immature cretins and did little to help that by trying to outdo Britney Spears with their

Rapture

provocative dress (or lack of it). I felt like an observer behind a one-way mirror at a human behavioural research lab. I studied the body language, listened to snippets of conversations, fascinated by my front-row seat. They would descend on the bar at about seven and the carnage usually started at eight o'clock. Special offers of two-for-one drinks and vodka pitchers were a huge hit. The goal was simple—intoxicate yourself as much as possible as quickly as possible. Some guys didn't buy a pitcher for a few buddies. Instead, they bought one and stuck in a straw. I loved drinking, but this was binging like I'd never seen before. You can't work in that kind of atmosphere and not be affected by it. I soon developed tactics so I could drink on the job. I'd under-pour the vodka to keep the stocks up and then fill the pitchers full of ice so there would be leftover Red Bull. I would then concoct a pint of the stuff for myself and sip it out back every time I went to empty the glass washer. It was the only way to survive the constant manic clamour of customers craving more alcohol. Abuse would be hurled if you passed up someone who had been waiting too long for their next drink.

Occasionally, someone would buy me a drink which according to bar rules I could have after the shift, as long as I notified the manager and printed the receipt. This system led to my next plan. I started printing receipts for bar tabs pretending that a whisky and coke on it had been bought for me by the customer. This worked like a charm. I realised

The Second Lap

how easy it was just to fall into a numb daze, never getting drunk on the job but always keeping the alcoholic-buzz-level nicely topped up. Others tried it too, but I was a master. If there was a way to sneak in a shot of vodka or a sly gin and tonic, I found it. We would take five minute breaks during the evening to have a cigarette and try to draw it out as much as possible. If you were a smoker, you got time to hang in the alley and get away from it, non-smokers got less time off!

The work days meshed together in a blur with nothing productive happening in between. I felt it was my divine right on my days off to do what my customers did all week, drink. I'd get up, shower, and then have a late breakfast or lunch. A few cans of beer usually followed before I figured out where the day would take me. A trip to an American-style burger restaurant in chic Barnes where Polly worked was a good time with free food and beer whenever she felt generous. Then we would pick up Trev and Kaisa on our way back and talk until late at some bar.

I didn't hate my life, but I needed to fill it up and give it more meaning. I was no longer the new kid on the block. What I craved was stability and the love of a good woman to share my days and nights. I was envious of Trev and Polly for what they had. That would change over time as their relationship became more volatile. However, I believed that I was a decent guy and had a lot to offer any girl who would have me.

Rapture

Looking too hard for something can be a curse because you see things that aren't there. It took one introduction from Frenchie to her friend Mischa and I was smitten. I didn't just fancy her, I went gaga. Mischa was tall and had luminosity about her. She was pale in a classic way and had a pixie smile and a face that was framed with choppy strands of mousy brown hair that made her look like she had just woken up from a nap. She looked like she had just gotten *out* of bed, and I wanted to take her *to* bed. I felt ridiculous. How could I exude a calm exterior when inside the butterflies were using my stomach as a punching bag? She came in most weekends and we talked as I made her French Martinis. I latched onto someone in the hope that she would stop the drifter in me. She made me want to be a more sober individual and a kinder person. Trev warned me that I was going too fast, but I never listened. How could this not work out? I thought that by being a good guy I would prevail and be her knight. The saddest thing about my desire for her was I knew that there was no spark there, but in earnest I pushed on. I hoped that my enthusiasm would overcome the lack of chemistry and I could win her heart. We became friends, went to parties together, flirted endlessly and cared for each other at least platonically. I was more in love with the idea of being in love with her than anything else.

I had been plucking up the nerve to ask her out for weeks, filling journals with sonnets and long-winded prose and musings, not at all living in the real world.

The Second Lap

Then *she* called. I interpreted the call as her saying, *Hey are we going to go out or what?* I was enraptured! We would finally get our date. After I stopped bouncing off the walls, I panicked. What to wear, where to go, how to take it? Trev and I consolidated wardrobes in an attempt to find something outside of our grunge-chic collections. We settled on a boring ensemble of a safe looking sweater, pair of pants, and shoes he had that were a size too small. My feet would suffer, but they would take one for the team. I was a ball of nerves the whole day before the big night and fretted about every little detail.

For the location, I decided on a little gastro-pub called The Grove in a quieter part of Hammersmith. With its high ceilings and old wooden finish, it was perfect. We drank Pinot Grigio and ate fish and talked about everything and anything. I didn't want the night to end. But end it did and on a lukewarm note at that. There was no passionate kiss or lingering embrace at the door, and I should have cut my losses. But I didn't, I was blindly ploughing on, desperate for her to be my girl.

A few weeks later at a night club, Mischa suggested we meet for lunch on the following Sunday. So we had coffee and made small talk until she told me there was nothing between us other than a deep friendship. I saw it coming, but still I was crushed: the finality of it all, the absolute certainty that all hope was gone. I spent the afternoon in the park drying my tears and cursing myself for being a nice guy. The jerks always got the girl.

Rapture

I wasn't sure of myself as a young man at all and I spent a world of time wanting people to like me. I wanted to be everything to everyone without ever asking myself *what would make me happy?* I had no notion of what my role in life was. Did I have a role? Did it matter? Was I here just to pass time and give and give and give and get nothing in return? I did know one thing; I was going to get drunk at work that afternoon. In the weeks that followed, I found my binging mojo and started drinking on the bus into work. I had been in London for nine months and my frustrations had begun to get the better of me and, in the tradition of great alcoholic writers, my writing was suffering because I was coming home from work blitzed and passing out. This was not how it was supposed to be.

I started having episodes where I blacked out completely that really scared me. The first time it happened was after myself and my good South African friend Bruce went on a Sunday blowout. He was as crazy as I was, and after leaving *The Church*, Kings Cross, where a morning session was held every Sunday, we stumbled out into daylight. The Church really has to be experienced to be fully understood. It's a cavernous warehouse where cans of Aussie booze are sold in plastic bags and sawdust litters the floor to dry up spillages. The motto is, "If you haven't sinned, you can't be forgiven." Fosters beer, wet T-shirt contests and unashamed Antipodean excess ruled the day. It started early and finished early.

The Second Lap

I was now following in Rory's footsteps. It hadn't even ticked three o'clock and I could barely negotiate a straight line. The next fuelling stop was a pub called The Backpackers which had chairs designed for doing shots. You sat in the chair and a hot girl straddled you with a bottle of tequila or some other poison and poured it straight down. I didn't care about the hot girl. I cared about the alcohol. The drunker I got the less I hurt in my mind. I lost Bruce in all the carnage and had no idea how to get home. I couldn't move and barely remembered crawling up the street and literally lying down in the gutter. People were shouting at me to move and looking down at me to see if I was alive. Then the lights went out. When I woke I could feel pains in my ribs and inside my head. Peering into my vision stood a policeman who had arrived on the scene the night before and taken me back to the station to sleep it off. I had no idea where I was and to this day still don't. All I know is that he put me on a bus after a long discussion with the driver who in turn told me when we had reached my apartment. I alighted the bus and vomited into the nearest bin and went up to my room. I lay on my bed embarrassed and ashamed over what I had done to myself. I cried more than I had in a long time. I was losing my way, and the spiral was just going further downward.

After that scare, I cleaned up my act for a bit, but soon my memory of that night was replaced with anticipation of the next drink. I kept living fast and

Rapture

crashing out on buses and waking up in strange suburbs of London with no idea how to get home.

    I was working as a floor manager now in the restaurant part of the bar and it suited me more. I had moved to waiting tables for a change of perspective and was a natural. I charmed tips from punters and had organisational skills that made me a good leader. I was always picky about presentation and made sure that every knife and fork were in their right place and gleaming. The small details meant the most, and if you did it half-way on my watch, then you did it again and again until it was right. I might have been a raging alcoholic, but my attention to my customers never wavered. The extra cash was also good to pick up CD's or go to a good rock show. I stopped looking for love and had given up on ever finding someone for me. Then Alicia walked in the door.

16

Searching

IT WAS A crisp and clear March afternoon as Trev worked the bar and I the floor. We were talking at the drinks dispense area where he prepared my orders for the customers. It was a good arrangement because we weren't in each other's hair all the time. It put balance in our friendship. I don't think we've had a serious fight in the twenty years we have known each other and it's because we can both gauge the other so well. He knows when to kick my butt to get me going and I know when to tell him he is being too loud and annoying me. The service had been slow with nothing to write home about, but when she walked into the bar I could have dropped. The first words out of my mouth were, "I'm going to marry her."

Searching

She was tall, at least 5 9" with jet black hair that hung just above her waist. She took a seat in one of the booths and crouched with intense concentration over a magazine. Kerrang! to be exact. Now, Kerrang! was the bible for rockers back then with the best weekly coverage of any band worth their salt. I loved it. The only thing that surpassed the pile of beer cans in our flat was the pile of dog-eared Kerrang! magazines. Being an encyclopedia of rock myself I now had my opening.

"Hi there, what can I get you?"
"A diet Coke."
"Is that Kerrang you're reading?"
"Yeah, I'm in a band."
"Really? I'm a drummer."
"I play the bass. Can I order the tuna steak, please?"
"Sure, how would you like it cooked?"
"Rare, I'm French."

"Rare, I'm French." Those three words said it all. She didn't sound at all French in that *Inspector Clouseau from the Pink Panther* way, the stereotype that most people turn to when they think of a French accent. She came across with a hint of an English accent but nothing too discernible. Of course, the international intrigue only added interest to this mystery lady. Her friend soon joined her for lunch and I overheard snippets of conversation about a gig she had played recently. I hoped that there would be another gig that maybe I could get an invite to. After

The Second Lap

quickly paying the bill she was gone. I had no idea if she would come back or not, but I could hope.

Around the end of March and beginning of April, West London changes. The dreary dark nights are a memory and the evening light stretches lazily into a soothing dusk. The river Thames and the pubs that dot its banks become the place to be as beer gardens fill with thirsty after-hours office workers. Hammersmith has an abundance of drinking establishments, but our spot was always The Old Ship. Steeped in history dating as far back as 1722, it is a beautiful and spacious pub with an enormous lawn for a beer garden and a perfect view of the river. On any given day it was mobbed with young people sitting on the grass and drinking pints of beer. Trev, Sam, Frenchie, Mischa, and our revolving cast of bar staff always met there to catch up and get drunk on our evenings off. We talked nonsense and thought we were living the greatest times in our young lives. Time and responsibility were irrelevant, and if one of us didn't have much money, we shared amongst ourselves like a commune. It was all very liberating. After a week or so of being there almost every day, I spied Alicia. She was a drinker there too. I had passed her a few times on the Thames path with a mere nod and a hello as she was always with someone who, I would later find out, was her American boss. We still hadn't really talked since the "*Rare, I'm French,*" introduction, but I felt that the more I saw her the more she was warming to me. One particular evening when our camp was in an overly joyous mood, I

Searching

spotted her and a friend having a Bud by the pub's exit. I had been telling our group how enamoured I was by this girl and that I had started to notice her around more. I was then told that if I didn't go over and speak to her, I had no guts. Challenge accepted. The great thing about alcohol is that when consumed in correct proportions, it can give one what is known as Dutch courage. Named after Dutch gin invented to warm soldiers, they began drinking it for its calming effects before battle. My battle was of a different sort, but no less important in my mind. I approached her and her friend, who was introduced as Kiki, a quirky girl who was very funny and very direct. We talked music, work, and anything at all to keep the conversation moving. I liked Alicia. She had so many similar interests to mine. I finally asked her for her number on the pretext that I'd love to come and see her play. This was very true; I did want to see her band in action, but I also wanted something more. Kiki then blurted out Alicia's age, thirty-one. I think Kiki was trying to embarrass her, and I laughed. I was twenty-four years old, so I could be cheeky and rub it in. She was one foot in the grave. After they left, I went back to my friends who were incredibly curious as to how it had gone. As I told them how great she seemed, I received a simple text message from her: 'I hope my friend didn't put you off with my age.' I remember my even simpler reply: 'We've only just begun.'

Another two weeks passed and one Sunday morning at Frenchie's, the usual suspects started

The Second Lap

to come to life at her apartment and shake off the liver destruction from the night before. The day was laid out in front of us like a red carpet. The question was, how much trouble could we get into? Frenchie pulled out a block of hashish the size of a chocolate bar and announced that hash brownies would be the order of the day. No protest there. She expertly dissolved the hash in large spoonfuls of vodka before mixing it into a huge bowl of brownie mixture. It was not the first time she had done this. We had been warned that each brownie would pack enough punch to lay down a rhino for the afternoon. Before we decided to leave, I got a text from Alicia asking if I wanted to meet for a drink at the Ship. I responded to her, 'Sure, but I won't get there for at least another two hours.' Grabbing our batch of illegal cakes, we made tracks to the pub, nibbling them slowly on the way so as not to tranquillise ourselves too early on. By the time I met Alicia our brigade was giggling out of control. Every time a bartender collected a glass from the table, we would erupt into one giant coalesced gut-laugh. I told Alicia our secret and she found it amusing, even though she didn't partake. As the evening progressed, less and less made sense. Anyone who had eaten the brownies was on their way to another planet. Suddenly, two Japanese girls appeared at our table and announced that they had been walking London all day and were starving. They pulled up a seat and a conversation started: where they came from, what brought them to London and so on. I am convinced

Searching

they knew what was going on with the hash cakes. It had to be obvious to anyone observing us, right? Seven people hunched around a table unable to keep a straight face and being generally stupid *had* to be a giveaway. It was that train of thought that led us to a chorus of *"help yourselves"* when they asked if they could each have a brownie.

Meanwhile, I'm talking to Alicia and our faces are moving closer together and while her body language is suggesting that I kiss her, I'm so stoned I can't read any of the signals. Nevertheless, I bite the bullet, lean over and kiss her awkwardly. Luckily, she responds, and the crew lets out a cheer of relief that Mally is finally getting some action. During the prolonged kissing my concentration breaks as I hear raised voices with an undercurrent of panic. It's the Japanese girls. They hadn't a notion that the brownies were spiked, and now they are losing their minds. I had seen this many times over the years. Once we reassured them that there was nothing to worry about and that surrendering to it was the best course, they seemed to take it on board and ride the magic bus. They got really into it before long and hung around with the guys discussing with gusto whatever subject came up. I was mentally starting to drift in a bad way and sensed that Alicia had seen and heard enough to want to get out of there.

We agreed that the time had come to make our move, so we bailed to get a pizza and a beer at a restaurant she frequented. She ate a pizza and I just stared at my beer bottle. I'm sure she was thinking,

The Second Lap

Great, another stoned loser who just wants to get wasted all the time. I couldn't have argued with her either; that's all I seemed to do. That was our first night together and it was not the ground-moving experience it could have been due to my intoxication, but waking beside her the next morning felt right. Her small bedsit was a haven from the relentless partying and revolving door lifestyle of the apartment I shared with my friends. I liked the peace of her place, and her album collection mirrored mine to a T. We had just met and had so much to share with each other. I didn't question it in my head like I had done with other relationships. This time I'd follow my heart and see where it would lead me.

17

Rainbows

THE BEGINNING OF a relationship is bliss, needing to see the other desperately at every moment of being apart. The suggestive messages passed on phones or email, planning concerts or going to movies. I'd spend an occasional night at her place and when I wasn't working the evening shift, I brought her expensive French wine to impress her and show her I was more than just a party guy. Her company filled a part of me that had long been neglected. She was more mature than most of the women I'd met which also meant she knew what she wanted out of life. She was spectacularly opinionated and upfront on just about any topic. She had moved from Paris to London five years previously for a guy and it hadn't worked out. She worked a string of personal assistant jobs

The Second Lap

before landing a good gig at a renowned soft drinks company where she looked after the vice-president of communications. We ran in different circles and I'm not sure she was too excited about hanging out with the friends I had at the time, although she loved Trev. We met musicians at bars and searched music shops for CD's and bargains and spoke of previous failed relationships. Both of us had been hurt in the past. I had grown tired of the games people played and wanted to be upfront about everything. Alicia kept more to herself out of fear that I would just up and leave her someday; we had work to do. Things at my own apartment were becoming unhinged and I buried myself in books. I devoured anything I could get my hands on. I discovered the works of Howard Zinn and Noam Chomksy, great minds with purpose and intent who changed the scope of the world. It was Zinn especially, whose writing and activism in the U.S. civil rights movement, that struck me most. I trawled the markets for cheap and interesting reads. I found some great William S. Burroughs titles and more books by my favourite writer since my early teens, Charles Bukowski. Books have the greatest ability, along with the healing art of listening to or playing music, to take me away to a different land. The power of literature, coupled with my imagination, can transpose me to dive bars, civil rights rallies, the heart of corrupt totalitarian governments, and other complex historical circumstances that provoke me to ask myself what I would do in a given situation.

Rainbows

I found I needed to disengage from where I lived. I loved Trev dearly, but the constant fights between him and his girlfriend did nothing to settle my nerves. Doors got slammed and broken, screaming matches at all hours of the day and night left me walking on eggshells.

The drug situation was worsening too and reached a point of madness when Kaisa came home from work with a rock of crack cocaine. Cocaine has long had a reputation as a millionaires' drug. It's pricey and seen as something that high-end bankers and business men abuse. It was readily available in London and lots of people I knew did it. Crack, on the other hand is a cancer in a community. Across the world, any television report you see on it is centred on a bunch of poor folks with no teeth and dead eyes who would do *anything* for a score. The wave of addictive bliss that washes over you when you smoke it ensures that you would sell your own mother for a hit.

Kaisa had worked for some sleazy Egyptian restaurant bosses who according to her were up to all sorts of dark deeds behind closed doors. On this night they ordered her to go and pick up some crack for them. She had done as she was told, but she made sure to break off a chunk as compensation for her troubles. The two Egyptians were none the wiser.

So there she sat on our sofa with this rock of crack in her hand. Kaisa and Polly were excited at this score, but Tom, a friend of Polly's, and I were nervous. This was a crossroads moment. My mind

The Second Lap

fast-forwarded ten years, imagining living in a junkie slum where I'd rewind and pinpoint this as the moment where it all went wrong. But even with that futuristic nightmare in my head, the lure of the unknown appealed too much.

Kaisa prepared the crack paraphernalia. With a rubber band, she secured a square of tin-foil over the mouth of a pint glass that was filled a third of the way with water. Pin-holes were pricked through the top of the foil towards the lip of the glass, not too many holes, but just enough to create an air filter. On the diametric opposite she sliced a small slit that we would smoke the fumes through. Once it was ready she carefully tipped burned cigarette ashes on the pin-holes letting it slowly smoulder out. She placed the crack on the ashes and hovered a lighter over the rocks as she inhaled. The first thing that hit me was the smell—pungent and scorched.

I took a hit next. Smoking the drug allows extremely high doses of cocaine to reach the brain very quickly, bringing an intense and immediate high. Within seconds I was floating in the air without a care in the world and thirty seconds later was greedily awaiting my next turn. The trouble with all drugs is that the first high will never be found again, but you keep taking the hit, smoking the score, inserting the needle, searching for that virgin experience. I was immediately giddy and animated, hugging Tom and telling him he was the greatest. Every inhibition was gone: the crack-induced honesty amongst the four of us was alarming. I

Rainbows

chain-smoked cigarettes in between hits and just wanted more and more of it. When it was finished, we drank beers and smoked four packets of cigarettes before walking to the shop to buy more. If there had been some crack in the house the next day I would have, without hesitation, lit up again. I am forever grateful that there wasn't, as I would have taken a dive from which I may never have resurfaced.

I needed to get out of that house. I talked to Alicia and considering how much time I already spent at her apartment, we decided that I should move in with her. I saw her in my future for the rest of my life and was ready to commit to living with a woman for the first time ever. We were happy, young, and in love. The madness would finally end.

I don't think I'd ever been more happy or sure of something. Living together was effortless. The chicken take-out dinners that had sustained me for months were replaced with home-cooked meals. Alicia was a revelation in the kitchen. Being French, she taught me about the simplicity of using seasoned ingredients to make a meal sing. I loved the care and preparation she put into everything she created. It made meals more than just an occasion to stuff my face—it made them a wonderful ritual.

Growing up in Ireland, I loved the rustic food of stews and potatoes, but by travelling the world my palette had become more varied and curious. Domestic bliss suited me just fine. I also left Bar 38 for a barman's position at a local pub called The Stonemasons Arms.

The Second Lap

The Stonemasons was *the* London gastro-pub in the days before it became a by-word for expensive foreign beers and over-priced food. The foodie revolution would grow in the decade that followed thanks to the huge influence of this independent pub. I wanted to be on their team and had hassled them for months to give me a shot when they had an opening. I got to know the place through Trev and on our breaks from Bar 38 we would go there and knock back a few Leffe beers and whine about our jobs. Funky artwork adorned the walls and gave local artists a chance to showcase their talent and maybe make a few extra bucks by selling their wares. The appearance of the place was rustic and minimal, a few lamps here and there, old wooden chairs and tables and a menu that changed daily.

My first contact there was Krist, a one-of-a-kind Swede whose outlook and opinions have yet to be equalled. His views were militant and controversial, and he would spout the strangest things. Example: customer comes in and orders a pint of orange juice and lemonade. When paying he asks:

"How much?"

"£2,50,"

"That's ridiculous,"

"Ridiculous drink, ridiculous price, my friend."

He called everyone *my friend,* even guys who got on his nerves. When he said it, you had to wonder whether he was being genuine or sarcastic. He loved testing people and kept a cool head most of the time. When he lost it though, it was best to get below

Rainbows

the parapet. Plates and cutlery were thrown, offices thrashed, and doors punched when a situation got the better of him. His volatility left a lot to be desired, but his honesty and outlook drew me to him. He didn't suffer fools and neither did I. One day I was in there on the lam from Bar 38 and he sat in front of me sliding a free Leffe across the table and said, "Mal, my friend, they need you. Not just anyone, man. They need *you*."

There was stiff competition for jobs at the Stonemasons. Everyone wanted to work on that team. There was no uniform to wear, we picked the music that was played and the food was dynamite thanks to a bunch of Brazilians who cooked as hard as they partied. All the staff were proud to work there.

Now I was on the team. From the off, it was the perfect job. The services were insanely busy, the clientele high rollers who knew what they wanted. I alternated between working the floor in the day time and the bar at night. We drank on duty and when the Brazilians finished in the kitchen at 10:30 P.M., we would all meet for a few minutes in the changing rooms downstairs to hoover up lines of cocaine, the bar staff rotating in turns to get high. I'd be pouring a beer for a customer and get a tap on the shoulder from a wide-eyed bartender, who'd just had a hit, motioning for me to go down. I would then descend to the changing room, walk into a cacophony of Portuguese discussion, snort up what we called train tracks (two long parallel lines of cocaine) in quick

The Second Lap

succession and then get back to it. Alicia knew about the drinking. The cocaine use I kept to myself.

The Stonemasons had a sister pub in Chiswick, The Pilot, right beside our old flat. It was there that Trev and I met Dave 'The Captain' Lightfoot and Will 'The W' Mace. Two best friends from Brisbane, Australia, they had been cut from the same cloth as Trev and I in every way possible. They were smart, partied hard, funny, grunge-heads, and genuine. Over the years we got loaded, went to shows, laughed, cried, and were generally inseparable. Dave and Will had a generosity of soul and gave us much more than any other friends we had ever met. Trev and I were always a duo and rarely did anyone get behind the veil of what made our relationship so special. We loved them deeply from early on and a bond stronger than brothers would form between the four of us, taking turns in carrying the other when times got tough. When his relationship with Polly eventually imploded, Trev managed to get a job at The Pilot working with the Captain. He moved into one of the rooms above the pub, and so began the most dazed period in our lives. For me, living with Alicia kept me out of the eye of the storm those times when it got really out of hand.

When the moment to meet the family came I was as ready as I could be. Going to France was a big deal for me. Since my pre-teen days of French exchange students coming to Cloghan, I couldn't have imagined a more foreign country. Eating snails and frog legs, drinking copious amounts

Rainbows

of red wine, smoking Gitanes cigarettes, all the stereotypes awaited me as our Eurostar whooshed us under the tunnel into the rolling hills of the French countryside. Holding her hand and staring out the window like the cat that got the cream, I felt very blessed. How long I had hankered to visit Paris. Now I was doing it alongside the woman with whom I hoped to spend the rest of my life. Alicia's parents were separated and lived far apart, her mum in the west of the country a few hours' drive and her dad in a care-home in the Paris suburbs. Various aunts and uncles lived with their families in western Paris near the famed Château de Versailles, Viroflay to be exact. I had been memorising how to say 'hello' and 'pleased to meet you' in French for a few weeks in the hope of impressing positively on them.

Her family was a mixed bunch of strong personalities and opinions; it would take me a long time to understand the dynamic of aunts and uncles, those who got on well and those who didn't. And deciphering the family was made doubly difficult by the mere fact these people were French. Through my Irish eyes, it was not easy to interpret the nuances and subtleties that defined their relationships; they seemed more closed off, pretentious almost. In Ireland we let it all hang out and went down to the pub for a few beers and laughed at ourselves. The French had long dinners that were alive with debate and spectacular opinion. Even ten years on, deciphering the dynamics in this culture can be challenging.

The Second Lap

That first visit was all fun, touring the jaw-dropping monuments and smaller charms that make Paris, for me, the most beautiful city in the world. The Eiffel Tower, Versailles castle, Notre Dame, Montmartre, and the Louvre were the obvious attractions. But I was also drawn to the network of quaint streets buzzing with bistros and vibrant culture. I adored it. Alicia took me to places where famous writers and artists hung out, pointing to cafés she and her friends had frequented in her youth, smoking and talking late into the cool nights of yesteryear.

Showing myself to be the tourist that I was, I snapped pictures furiously. Alicia guiding me around postcard-picture monuments during the day with our nights spent drinking *pastis* and eating *foie gras* with her family at some gathering or another. It was never boring. Engrossing discussions entertained me right through until dessert and cheese. I could barely make out a word of the language, but I was content to immerse myself in this romantic life.

We returned to Hammersmith where I loved my job. I decided to start thinking of it as a career. I had a way with customers and could deal with all types of people with ease. If I needed to keep a punter happy, then I plastered on a fake smile and got it done. On the other foot was my butt-kicking shoe. That got used from time to time too. I have served thousands of people over the years, many of whom hit the pub to imbibe and step out of their skin. Here's a basic tenet, derived from all those years behind a bar: if a

Rainbows

person is easy going when they're sober it normally means they're easy going when they're drunk. The alternate to this is the person who is an ignoramus when sober becomes a complete jerk after a few tipples.

My rules were simple. If you have no respect for the people serving you, then take it somewhere else. I have been abused and called many names in my time; it took a few years to develop a thick skin to alcohol-induced abuse, but I got used to it.

By now I saw it more as a serious job, and when I looked back to when I started as a glass collector, I was proud of the upward trajectory of my life. Things were rolling nicely for Alicia and me. Our first Christmas together was approaching and we had not only survived, but thrived, over the previous nine months. We would celebrate at a huge gathering with her family in Versailles. Sticking to tradition, the *fête* was to be held on Christmas Eve.

18

"What I want for Christmas, only you can give me"

THAT WAS THE response I got after a few weeks of prodding Alicia over Christmas presents. It was either the most opaque or the most obvious hint; I wasn't sure which. I thought hard about it for three days. On the third day I decided I would ask her to marry me. It was a gamble. If my radar wasn't picking up her signals, then it was going to be embarrassing. It was time for my undercover mission to begin.

The first thing I did: while she was in the shower, I found a ring of hers and tried slipping it on my fingers until I had a fit—my little finger. That would be my size reference. Then I consulted my budget. This was love, and the budget had to budge. I spent a week's wages at a local jeweller's on a nice little ring that fit snugly on my pinkie. Now I had to

"What I want for Christmas, only you can give me"

hide it. I bought a red cash box about the size of a biscuit tin that had a lock and key. I opened the jeweller's box holding the ring and attached it to the inside of the cash box with some double-sided tape. When Alicia opened the cash box, the ring would be glistening back at her. I then locked the cash box and taped the key to the top. Then I wrapped it in some cheap Christmas wrapping. I gave her the package about a week before Christmas. It drove her mad not knowing. She knew three things: it was light, sounded like it was made of metal, and was plainly shaped.

A French guy named Vinnie had been tending bar with me for a couple of months. One evening I asked him in the most roundabout way, how would one propose, in French, to a woman, if one just happened to be interested in marrying said woman. He didn't catch my ruse and once he told me, I wrote down his phrasing and practised hard so I'd be ready to get it right in front of twenty-five or so of my (possibly) new in-laws.

This time we took Alicia's trusty blue Renault Clio through the Channel tunnel for the trip to Paris. It was cheaper and allowed us to bring gifts and enjoy a road trip. Rock music blared on the stereo and all that rang through my head was *'accepter tu de devenir ma femme?'* It was a mantra that I rehearsed in my mind so many times that I almost blurted it out on at least three occasions. But somehow I managed to keep my mouth shut the entire trip.

The Second Lap

Arriving in Paris, preparations were in full swing. Her aunt and uncle had the biggest house so they hosted each year. We guests were responsible for one dish or item: cheese, wine, dessert, salads, salmon, oysters, and bread all had to be considered and it was organised with impeccable precision. Our banquet would be memorable for more than just the food.

When Christmas Eve came, we convened at their house in Versailles which was decorated magnificently. The dinner table looked better than any restaurant I had been in or worked for; the attention to detail was sublime.

French dinners are long affairs—the Irish/English fashion of wolfing the meal down and hitting the beer does not happen. If feasting is a two hundred metre dash for us, for the French it's a marathon. The *apéritif* is first. Over nibbles, whisky, beer, *pastis,* Martini, and gin, kisses are exchanged and personal news caught up on. That night, the subsequent conviviality completely took away my nervousness about my proposal. The fact that my spoken French was still very poor didn't matter. After *apéritif* the men repaired to the garage to open the evening's oysters, smoke cigars, and drink *pastis*. My oyster cracking skills were less then desired. It took three attempts with an oyster knife—a special blunted knife made for the job—before I could open one without almost slicing my hand. Watching my fumbling with the shells, the men made good-natured fun of the Paddy.

"What I want for Christmas, only you can give me"

When the starter came, I didn't know where to begin. There was a specific bread for the *foie gras*, another bread for the salmon, and a different wine to drink with each. I became slightly frustrated and embarrassed by everyone trying to interject themselves into my perplexed state, only to realise they were genuinely trying to help me. What was I doing by attempting to marry into this foreign family?

Course after course appeared. My stomach groaned by the time we had finished the main and started into *fromage* and dessert.

After all the plates were cleared, we picked our presents from under the tree and gave them to each person. It resulted in a pile of about five or six parcels apiece. Midnight was approaching fast and as Alicia started opening her stack I made her promise that mine would be the last. Perfumes and soaps were piled up in front of her when she finally made it to the box. Shaking it and looking thoroughly bewildered, she ripped off the paper to find the key taped to the top. As she inserted it into the lock, I got down on one knee. She opened it and saw the ring. In shaky French and in front of her entire family, I asked her to marry me. She threw her arms around me and screamed *yes*! The eruption of joy and congratulatory hugs were overwhelming. I had to share this wonderful news with my own family. But when I called my mum and told the McLoughlin household my news, she sounded reserved. They were happy, but... . Nevertheless, still overjoyed, I

The Second Lap

sent a block text to all of my contacts. In return my phone popped and blinked with well-wishes for the remainder of the night. Later in the evening, I talked to several friends on the phone outside of the house, away from the noise.

It was two A.M. when one of Alicia's uncles stormed out of the house with his wife and son in tow. After hanging up the phone and going back in, I discovered that there had been a slight difference of opinion.

Before we knew it, four days had passed and we were driving back to London. On the way we agreed that Ireland would be the best place to get wed. My parents could organise a lot of the details for us.

First port of call in London was The Pilot for a pint of decent Guinness. I loved my French red wine, but nothing beat a pint of the black stuff. Trev was working and I wasted no time in asking him to be my best man. Once that was settled it was time to pick a date. Serendipitously, November 23rd, 2003 suited everyone. We locked it in and started saving money. I kept busy at the pub and Alicia was working for a new drinks company and excited to be doing so. We moved to a bigger place that was *ours* together. It had a beautiful garden and was quiet. Good-bye bedsit.

We had been together less than a year and would be getting married the following November. I was twenty-five years old with my whole life mapped out in front of me. What's the saying? *Man plans, God laughs.*

"What I want for Christmas, only you can give me"

My entire family put their all into helping us: mum and dad would buy the cake, my sisters Susan and Alison made calls and organised like fiends; Simon would be my groomsman and Sean, the youngest of the family, would sit there and look adorable. The French contingent booked flights and impressed us when fifteen of them landed in Dublin two days beforehand.

A few friends from London would make the trip too. The W, The Captain, and Krist jumped at the chance to get wasted on my native soil and practice their *faux* Irish accents on unsuspecting women.

The wedding day itself was a world of joy. I felt completed in all the ways a man should be. My usual garrulousness was replaced with a short speech that choked me up as I looked at my bride. Alicia was beautiful. My friends stared back at me from the guest tables and our French family danced and drank into the early hours. The whole week of being back home reinforced the importance of family and friends. We are not creatures of solitude. Our gathering and sharing of good times and low times is what makes humanity remarkable. It's a shame we don't do it always—it takes weddings and funerals and catastrophes to bring out the goodness in us. The small acts of kindness bestowed on me as I transitioned into life as a husband inspired me to be the best partner I could be.

I would have to tame the partying ways a bit because both Alicia and I knew, without having ever discussed it, that the natural progression for

The Second Lap

us as a couple was to start a family. Both of us respected marriage and honouring our union with a beautiful child would bring everything full circle. We decided to waste no time in trying. I was walking on air; nothing could dent my exuberance. Being married brought a new-found maturity to the way I approached life. I was taking more responsibility at the pub and had moved up to assistant manager after briefly taking on management duties when my boss was on vacation. I found that the trust placed in me elevated my mindset to one of inner belief. When someone believes in you, it's impossible not to raise one's game and reciprocate that trust. The people who worked under me appreciated my style. I was not dictatorial like some bosses I had worked under. I was unafraid to get my hands dirty, and I was fair. Maybe too fair sometimes, but I was on a learning curve.

After three or four months of trying, Alicia became pregnant with our first child. I was in our new living room having a beer after a busy afternoon when she went into the bathroom to do a pregnancy test. When she returned with her announcement, the feeling in my legs disappeared. I tried to stand up but couldn't manage it—total paralysis of my legs and somersaults of euphoria in my mind. We hugged, laughed, cried, and tried to take it all in. There would be many routine scans and doctors' confirmations to come, but that very first shared moment, just the two of us, was magical. The realisation that the love we had for each other would bring a new

"What I want for Christmas, only you can give me"

life into the world and our responsibilities would extend beyond just us was wonderful—and a tad bit terrifying. Would I be a good dad? That was the only question I asked myself. Did I have it in me to take a child's hand and guide him or her through the labyrinth of life?

19

Seed to Seedling

DYLAN CAME INTO the world on Friday, December 10th, 2004. Arriving home from my pub on the Wednesday beforehand, Alicia and I were settling into our bed when movement, unlike any other before it, signalled the baby was ready, almost. Contractions stayed slow and steady and took us into Thursday evening. Phone calls to parents and bosses were made and Alicia's Mum arrived on the scene that very day. Thursday night was more of the same and Friday morning was hospital time.

The baby had moved but now refused to budge. Alicia had suffered through two days without sleep and was weak; so the doctors injected her with Syntocinon to induce movement. The drugs they administered sent his heartbeat plummeting and

Seed to Seedling

the monitor strapped to Alicia's belly relayed this all back to us. I was worried and sleep-deprived. I started seeing flashes of ghost-like light out of the corner of my eyes. It would cross the room and sweep through the air before being sucked out the window. Alicia was hurting and still it dragged on. After pushing more drugs to speed up the labour his heart beat went into free-fall. I screamed out the door to the doctor who bolted up the hallway. My words were bordering on aggressive when I told him to "Get my boy out NOW!!" There was no argument. He knew it was not going to be a natural birth and action was needed immediately. He threw some surgical scrubs across the room at me and started pushing the bed with a nurse. I followed, wheeling a monitor of some sort with various cables attached. Once in the surgery room, it was organised chaos. Nurses and anaesthetists streamed in and assumed positions. I stood by Alicia, tightly holding her hand. She was doing so great, but time had taken its toll. We both longed for it to be over, Alicia probably the most. They asked us if we wanted music. *No thanks, just our son please.*

When they delivered him after some speedy work, we waited for the sound of his cry. Nothing came. He was placed on the table to be cleaned and checked and after twenty to thirty seconds that clung to the air almost indefinitely, he wailed and let us know he was alive and with us. The feelings and the emotions since that very moment remain the same: there is no greater joy in the world than being a father.

The Second Lap

As I held him in my arms, I was flooded with the realisation that I had to clean up my act. It wasn't a miracle of feeling reborn myself; I drastically needed to alter my perception and my habits. Change doesn't come at once; it requires building and time, patience and will. For the moment, I would settle for sleep. Becoming a dad transcends all. I tried to recall my life before this and wonder what I did with my time. I was a young father by my friends' standards, but age is never an accurate gauge for how one feels in life.

Working in the bar industry became tougher after Dylan's birth. I missed him terribly on the nights I worked late and would take over the next bottle feed at night after Alicia spent her day and evening with him. I loved that period when the world slept and he and I shared some blissful moments with nothing more than the moon peering through the blinds for company. I would tell him stories about how much beauty and adventure lay ahead of him when he would become a man. How much he would achieve by just being himself, his wonderful, bright self. He was a magical addition to our world and he rippled through our entire lives and the lives of our families. He was the first grandchild on either side of the family and with that honour came presents and visits from both sides. The birth of a child has the power to bring out the very best in people because in it we see the chance to encourage a life to the fullest. Children are like blank canvasses onto which we project our own hopes and dreams. We look at

Seed to Seedling

them with awe and secretly whisper advice to them in hopes they will not make the same mistakes we ourselves have made in our lives.

Most people I know harbour some regrets about a past encounter or a crossroads in their lives where if they had the chance to go back, they would have taken the other road. There was a film in the late nineties called *Sliding Doors* starring Gwyneth Paltrow, and even though it was a run-of-the-mill schmaltzy romance piece, the concept was based around *what if?* The main character misses her train just as the doors close and from there on in we see the parallel lives she follows because of her tardiness. It's not rocket science and it's certainly not *Taxi Driver,* but it is the burning question. *What if?* Does a part of us yearn to change something in the past? Yes. It is a waste of time to wonder if the grass is greener on the other side or spend time counting the things you haven't got, as opposed to what you have got. But we all go there sometimes.

Foremost on my mind was climbing the ladder in the pub trade. After years of hard graft, my company rewarded my loyalty and gave me my own pub to manage, The Pilot of all places—close to home. A few months later they pulled the carpet from under me and sold it to a money-grabbing company with hundreds of pubs. Things changed overnight; gone was the freedom to be creative in an increasingly generic business. Rules and red tape landed in its place. Working for the big guns had no advantages

The Second Lap

and when I met my new boss something inside me hardened.

Gordy was a sour-faced runt of a man with a big belly, Napoleon Complex, and zero empathy. He was a person who looked at the figures on a spreadsheet at the end of the month and wanted more. Other factors didn't matter. If you weren't making money, you were surplus to requirements. My place was doing well, but I had a bigger vision for it. Gordy thought changing absolutely everything would ensure continued success. Months passed and sales dropped. Meetings were had as to why this year had not been as profitable as the last. My response was simple: if it's not broken, don't fix it.

We had pioneered the foodie pub revolution, and this guy breezed in and took a wrecking ball to all of it. Life for me started to unravel in my mind. I had this wonderful child and an amazing wife, but I couldn't sleep. I ate less and less and drank more and more. Meanwhile, Gordy sent in spies to watch us all. Reports would come back to say he had a witness to my drinking a beer at ten o'clock on Friday night. He called unannounced and sat in dark corners observing for entire days. My assistant manager had a breakdown and left because she couldn't handle it and soon everyone was leaving.

Hate is a strong word; it really is. It gets thrown around a lot because we hate such a guy if he is rich and handsome, or some girl because she is beautiful and popular. But this sort of hate really

Seed to Seedling

is an exaggerated form of envy. If you look at the synonyms for hate; despise, resent, loathe, abhor.... it's strong stuff. I felt for the first time in my life that maybe I was capable of detesting someone this much. When he left the pub in his car, I sometimes daydreamed of a bolt of lightning striking it and frying him to ash inside. I thought of the smarmy grin being wiped off his face through some act of karmic or cosmic equilibrium. Because I believed in God, I felt guilty. I didn't believe in hating someone. It's not what I think we should be about or *are* about. Looking at the surface of something is the easiest way to dislike or *hate* it.

I had a beautiful son who kept me going through this tough period and has every day since, a little body totally dependent on me. Gordy was a married man with no kids. He had power, depending on your definition of it, a big car and probably a hefty bank balance. But maybe he and his wife couldn't have a child. Maybe the fact he had a bit more weight on him than the average guy was a medical issue and he suffered when no one was looking. I moved away from my thoughts of ill will and felt sorry for him. Even when I resigned and he screwed me out of half my last salary cheque, I took it in stride. I wrote him a three-page letter letting him know that I had done my very best whilst there and that I would always strive to be a decent guy to get along with. The biggest crime for me would have been to bite the bullet and become another shill in the machinery of the commercial pub business. I had

The Second Lap

bigger and better plans for my life and it involved an offer from an old boss.

My friend Alex had been the manager at The Stonemasons and he jumped ship too when our pub got bought out. He got in with a group of guys whose ethos was the same as ours, individual pubs with character, great food, and good booze. Alex had the golden goose lined up for me and it didn't disappoint. Arriving for drinks at The Ladbroke Arms in Notting Hill on an autumnal Thursday evening, it was blatantly apparent that I was about to take a step up in the world. The pub exterior was adorned with colourful hanging baskets of flowers. Inside, small square tables edged together giving it a neighbourly feel, elbow room was at a premium. Staff buzzed around setting tables and chatting amiably with the customers, the dim lighting, wooden décor, and classic paintings lent it character. The place oozed class, money, and sophistication. Where I fit into it all, I wasn't quite sure of just yet. My experience at top level hospitality wasn't as extensive as most, and when Alex told his guys that a rookie was taking over they were understandably reserved. I was a little surprised myself and when I sat into a snug corner that evening, I asked Alex the same question, *"Why me?"* He replied that anyone could learn to run a business from a profit and loss point of view and that counting cash and pulling pints wasn't terribly complicated. But what I had in the personality department could not be taught. I had the charm and the people skills, apparently, to

Seed to Seedling

make customers feel special and at home. Flattered, I accepted the job on the spot. I trusted the guy and he had never done me wrong.

I started soon after, in early winter, and if I thought I had no time before, then I was in for a big surprise. With my more than decent salary came the responsibility. I was in charge of a large team of waiters, bar tenders, kitchen porters, and a chef who fancied himself as the boss, too. Schedules needed to be juggled and old staff habits broken. All that combined with getting to know the locals left time for little else. Each morning I'd drop Dylan at his nursery and cycle to work. Alicia was back working too and we rushed around a lot. We moved to a bigger place where Dylan could have a room of his own. Initially I eased off the booze to make sure I got a handle on the job. I was like a fish in water. It was effortless at times, and that was not good. Having something handed to me on a silver platter with a big bow around it would be a nightmare in the long run. The place functioned so well that I was raking in the cash, a salary and a share of the profits. The good times meant I returned to my old habit of drinking hard. With no spies hovering and a relaxed attitude to my running the place, I was up to my neck in alcohol before I even knew it. Scarily fast, in fact. It began with me and my paperwork. I'd arrive at eight thirty at the latest every morning, greet the kitchen team, and head for my office. I'd settle in and check my emails, consolidate all the cash and figures, deposit a few grand at the post office, make changes

The Second Lap

to the menu and talk to the chef about the specials, print the new menu, have a chat with the cleaner to make sure it was all tip-top and spick and span. The floor staff would arrive at ten and retrieve their instructions. After all of this concentrated effort, the reward portion of my brain signalled that it was time for me to have a little something. A half a pint of cider or Guinness and a cigarette at eleven o'clock was just the tonic. By opening time at twelve, a pint and a half would have been dispensed of with nary the bat of an eyelid. An air of entitlement pervaded my mentality. I thought that all my hard work in previous jobs justified my new attitude of abandon. Money devalued everything that had been precious. *Be careful what you wish for* —the cliché held true in my case because I had all the cash I needed but no real sense of who I was. Was I the same person I had always been? Undoubtedly yes. Was I living to my full potential and seeking the truth? No. I was in the limelight and that felt good, in the way I used to be as a drummer. There had always resided in me a conflicting nature: I could be incredibly depressed and self-destructive or I could be quite vain and egotistical. In my new role, I struggled to find a midway point on an emotional see-saw. Cocaine was as available as alcohol, the difference being that one was out in the open, the other was talked about in code. Rich clients equalled rich indulgences. Bankers, actors, musicians, everyone was shovelling the marching powder up their noses and it seemed completely normal. Wealthy people are not restricted

Seed to Seedling

by the same rules as poor or middle-class people. It's just a fact of life. Having money creates assorted short-cuts and get-out-of-jail cards. You do a favour for someone who knows someone or scratch the back of a guy who is connected and certain—let's just say illegal—activities can be made to disappear. I was as much a part of the problem as the millionaires because I condoned it. It was exclusive, dangerous, taboo. Thinking about it now, it's just plain stupid.

I came into work one morning after a mammoth binge that had me violently sick in the bin in my office. I couldn't even keep water down, so the staff called me a taxi to take me to the hospital. On the way over I shook and trembled and called an Alcoholics Anonymous automated number out of desperation. I had never considered AA before as I was functioning perfectly well and felt that the drinking gave me an edge in my work, but I had also never felt so deathly before. For the first time in my life, I said those three words to myself: *I'm an alcoholic*. Never even saw it coming. My phone rang. A guy who called himself Kevin came on the line and asked me about myself, my boozing habits, when I last took a drink. I lay on the back seat of the taxi crying my eyes out and begging him to help me overcome my horrors. He told me about a meeting near my home, so I told him I'd go as soon as I was out of hospital.

When I got to the emergency room, they took me in immediately and gave me a CT scan. After taking some Xanax I felt marginally better. Then the

The Second Lap

doctor arrived. He didn't bring terrible news, but he didn't bring good news either. The first diagnosis was kidney stones. That could be resolved with care and some medication. The second diagnosis was the real rub. He asked me how much I drank, I lied and told him half the amount. That amount still shocked him considerably. He took out the scan and held it up for me to see. Right there in my liver he indicated with a blue *Bic* pen (funny the things you remember) the start of cirrhosis. He didn't lecture me or admonish me. He gave me a look, one of sympathy and sadness at another young man slowly killing himself.

I had to quit or I would die. Even if I didn't die, but continued to drink, I would not be much of a father to anyone. It was a mega-shock, I promised myself I was done with drinking.

I spent the weekend recuperating and readied myself for a change of life.

20

Replenish

THE FIRST STEP of the long road to sobriety for me was AA meetings. I'd seen them portrayed on television, but I had never been.

"Hi, my name's Tommy and I'm an alcoholic."

"Hi, Tommy!"

I contacted the group in advance, and it was explained that I had to inform them that it was my first meeting. I was nervous that Sunday morning when I stepped in the door. I knew it meant a lot to Alicia and that she was proud of me for making the effort. I knew I had to change to hold onto my wife. We were married just three years and I had been absent in the marriage both physically and emotionally.

The meeting was held in a church a five minutes' walk from our apartment. Walking out the front door

The Second Lap

and over the railway bridge that faced our living room window, I swung a right at the bottom of the steps and down a little side street to the church. I climbed the wooden stairs to a room that served as a function room for after-service gatherings. I poked my head in the door and took a deep breath. *I can't do this*. I turned on my feet and briskly loped back down the stairs. Outside in the mild spring air I lit a Lucky Strike and pulled the smoke deep into my lungs. I needed just a little sip of something to get my courage up, but I had run out of road. I stubbed my smoke out against the brick wall and went back up. John was the first person I met; he had watched me go up and down the stairs hoping that I'd make the right choice. I was here wasn't I? He had been a weekend binge-drinker and did lots of nasty sexual stuff he wasn't proud of. His honesty was overwhelming; he seemed like a good person, though. People trickled in all eager to meet the new guy and I was having a decent time thinking, *this ain't so bad,* until people started telling their stories of drinking and recovery. I cried and cried and cried and cried and then some, listening to complete strangers talk about the lows they stooped to—their rock bottoms they called them. The families they had ruined and lost and the bridges they had incinerated and would never rebuild again. There is a deep empathy in a group like this because whilst all stories may vary in detail, fundamentally they are all the same. I had never been in some of the situations they had and vice versa, but I still had the

Replenish

chance to save my own life. I walked out of that first meeting feeling renewed and returned to work the following week with fire in my belly. I had been six months in the job, most of it a fog. Now I worked with class. I became a real pro in dealing with every troublesome aspect of the business, and there were many. I learned about myself and my colleagues and friends saw the changes in my attitude. My head was clear and I was less prone to the low patches that I had experienced on and off. Trev was beaming and encouraged me more than anyone. He still loved to party, but to see his soul-brother fighting back, and winning, was a special moment for him.

The first few months passed with no great difficulty because the impetus and motivation kept me between the rails. I attended the occasional meeting, but all the talk of drinking brought out cravings I could not repress. Six months into sobriety I could feel a familiar gnawing come back to haunt me. Everywhere I looked and everything I touched was alcohol-related. Tipsy, buzzed, and drunken people laughed it up under my nose at work and on my days off my friends just wanted to go to a pub.

All the will in the world is no good unless you have a plan. I had no strategy and yearned for just one more pint. Then I cracked. I had been sober nine months and my emotional distress levels were eating me alive. I wanted out of the pub business because it was too hard to avoid the temptation. To hell with it. I poured a pint of Heineken and took it to my office. I don't know how long it rested on my desk, drawing

The Second Lap

me in, tiny bubbles of condensation rolling down the ice-cold golden glass, my eyes growing misty, my heart-beat rising. It was like a magnet pulling me in. I called myself a weak good-for-nothing piece of crap. I pleaded at the glass, this inanimate object, to stop torturing me. The worst part of alcoholism is not the damage it does to others, though that is an immeasurable amount of damage. It's the helplessness and the shame, the inability to say no even when I so wanted to and the destruction of my self-esteem when I couldn't.

When I put the glass to my lips and drained it, I felt like a magic potion had been injected into me. I went straight upstairs, told my assistant manager I was leaving for a day or two and that I'd call. I then disappeared on a bender by myself for two days. During that time, I had plenty of conversations with God. I thanked Him for getting me back to drinking because that's who I was. That lasted until the alcohol kicked in hard and made me depressed and I cursed Him for being a deserter and not stopping me. I knew He was there listening and the fact He said or did nothing made me crazy.

Alicia was disappointed that I fell from grace. That's what I thought. I think she would probably have used the words devastated or distraught. I didn't know her pain like she knew her pain. We were keen to have a second child to give some company to Dylan which deflected some of the issue. Alicia had grown up an only child in a divorced household. I sensed she wanted a bigger family and

Replenish

a sibling for her boy and I agreed. It was not long before she was pregnant and a few months later the scans confirmed we would be having a girl. A boy and a girl, the king's choice of children who would have just under three years between them.

Due to the complications with Dylan, the doctors had advised another caesarean section by appointment. When nine months closed in they told us to come to the hospital at midday. We would have a baby before the evening. No ceremony at all and true to their time schedule that afternoon, August 3rd, 2007, Pearl was born. Named after Pearl Jam, she was a bundle of cuteness that made us complete.

Dylan was in awe of his baby sister as were we. This time it was harder, though. I was working and drinking out of control. Alicia was growing tired of my act, and when I came home at night exhausted, I would do the same as I had with Dylan. I'd feed Pearl, sleep maybe a few hours if I was lucky and then go back to work the next day, drinking whenever I had the chance.

I hid beer cans all over the house, vodka bottles in the shed. I had a hidden cellar in the pub with a stash of cans so I would always be close to alcohol. If I ran out or couldn't get my hands on something to drink, I panicked. I found a pub in the suburb where we lived that opened at eight A.M. I would leave for work early and arrive as they opened, drink four pints of cider in one hour and then hop back on my bike and cycle into work.

The Second Lap

My work got sloppy. I made mistakes with orders and became less patient with staff and customers. Nevertheless, my level of professionalism, outwardly at least, seemed on par to those around me, but inside I was falling to bits. Our Aussie friends Dave and Will had moved back home. I felt I needed to leave too.

Then Alicia had a brainwave: we should move to Paris. The kids would be near her family and would have a great system of schools. Alicia would be close to her cousins and I wouldn't have to work in a pub any more. I envisioned a sober future and a clean slate. After much negotiating and contractual fine print, we were set. I handed in my notice. I was sad to say goodbye to my team and also grateful to Alex for the chance, but I was done. Two years at The Ladbroke had broken me.

We packed our belongings and our mate Ade drove a van containing our life to France, following us in our car. Road trip.

My alcoholism and the details I describe here are only the scab of the wound. The gore below the scar tissue is something you can't see or truly grasp with just words on a page. Other addicts know what I mean. The families or friends of addicts might think they do and they do have an inkling and have suffered the consequences, but ultimately, it's a disease that only the sufferer can interpret.

Think about that word, *disease*. For example, what do I know about a person suffering from a malady that is bacterial or is eating away at their

Replenish

nervous system? Nothing outside of what a medical journal can tell me. But I know my own disease better than anything in my life. I understand its ability to make me crazy, to fill me with joy, to fill me with loathing, to tear down the walls of my sanity and make me want to hurt myself, to make my skin crawl and put my fist through the bathroom mirror at the sight of my disgusting face. My utter torture and powerlessness are not topics that merit bragging rights. On the contrary, it is a warning as to just how fast the life you think you are loving and getting through becomes a living nightmare. Where sickly dreams are blended into this foggy existence that nags at your every sinew. It's a beast waiting to be fed, a rabid dog needing to be put down because even though it wants to be stroked and loved, it will bite your hand off because it is too far gone to be saved. The line between life and death becomes less and less distinguishable.

Alcoholism has taken up over half my life and features in a lot of conversations I have with people who are often fascinated with it. I thought for sure I had it beaten by changing lifestyles. The greatest illusion was my believing it couldn't get any worse. It did; I went from drinking to survive, which was already hurting me deeply, to what I called a *suicide by instalment plan*. I was either going to come out of this sober, or in a pine box.

21

Arc

LIVING IN PARIS was not the same as visiting. The honeymoon was over. We moved to the nice, leafy suburb of Viroflay, just west of the city and bordering Versailles. It is still the place I call home, but in the early days I struggled to adapt. Everything was happening so fast. At first, we had nowhere to stay, so Alicia's Aunt Brigitte put us up until we found an old two-bedroom apartment. I knew none of the language and Alicia was working long hours right off the bat. Dylan needed to be enrolled in school and all the utilities needed to be connected, which in France is a chore. We had to become part of the system. I really hated the bureaucracy of it all in the beginning. It seemed that absolutely everything had to be made as difficult as possible, whether it was gas or electricity, phone

Arc

company or tax office. It took endless protocol and reams of paperwork to get a finger lifted. The clerks and secretaries appeared rude, defensive, and queuing didn't exist!!!

My first encounter with the queuing system could have led to my first murder. I went to the local supermarket and filled my basket, waited in line with the fifteen other baguette-holding moaners for the one cashier available. When a second cashier opened up, I proceeded in my orderly polite Irish manner, only for some snail-eating *Frog* to skip past me and put down his groceries first. Aghast, I had to remind myself to inhale or otherwise collapse from oxygen deprivation. The nerve of the dude.

I went back to the apartment where we were having a gathering over nibbles and drinks and recounted my story of the crazed queue jumper only to be greeted with laughter. This is what they do here, I was informed. I'd been in England for six years and that's not how it was done. One waited with a stiff upper lip and helped old ladies with their bags and maybe even helped carry them home too. By the looks of the French lot, they'd push an octogenarian in a wheelchair out of the way just to get back home a few minutes early. I was *not* impressed.

But I was in their country and I had moved there with gusto, so I would just have to suck it up. My role was to be a stay-at-home dad whilst Alicia started her new job. I felt so lonely I couldn't bear it. I took Dylan to school in the mornings and picked

The Second Lap

him up in the evenings and was proud of my little man the way he adapted. Pearl was in her pushchair still and we spent our time going to the park and getting used to the place. I cooked and cleaned and did laundry and loved spending time with the kids. But the disparity between being the host at the pub and suddenly having no one to talk to brought about intense isolation and sadness. Alcohol was my solution. When was it ever *not* my solution?

I craved interaction and could only feel something when I had a drink. If I had a meeting with the *crèche* or school about the kids, I would buy a beer or two and drink one just before. It helped me relax and took away my fear of speaking French. I could not do anything without Dutch courage. In order to contest a bank charge or to sign documents I would have to go to the park and drink at least two beers before walking in the door. I felt like Nicholas Cage in the movie *Leaving Las Vegas*. I was now drinking just to get by. I took very little pleasure in it any more. It was the proverbial monkey on my back. It felt like the only solace I could turn to.

I had to be wary of how much I spent because Alicia would notice discrepancies in the bank balance and with one wage it would be easy to spot. I drank my beloved Heineken, which was more expensive than other brands, until she started asking questions as to where ten euros here and there had gone. I'd bluff it and say the toilet was blocked and I had to buy an expensive product to clean it out. I eventually ran out of lies and shifted to drinking the

Arc

cheap stuff. I knew I was a low-life when I started buying the cut-price booze that alcoholics on the street drank. I became so adept at finding the best bargain that I could recite the various prices at all the different supermarkets. We're only talking cents here, small change. Marché U, the furthest shop away from home sold cans of Brauperle for forty cents. It was dirt cheap, tasted OK (after four of them), but it sold fast amongst the local bums. Most mornings it sold out early so I had to get there as soon as I dropped Dylan off at school. The next step up in alcohol quality was fifty-three cents at Ed, a local supermarket chain. It was my favourite, but if you're buying ten cans at a time it adds up. On the plus side, that shop was close by.

It was all part of the game, the scheming and calculating, drinking enough to get loaded but not too much so Alicia would smell it when she got home. When she did smell it, I would go on the offensive and actually convince her she was going crazy. I was so good that at times she really thought she was going mad. She deserved better than my duplicity. She deserved better after four and a half years of marriage, period.

Life was suddenly *different*, as if the fire had dimmed and neither one of us had the breath to kindle the dying embers. I was withdrawing and she was working hard to pay for everything. It would be a while before it would simmer to the top, but we carried on with our heads down. I adored my family and I wanted to get it together.

The Second Lap

Dylan was rocking school and Pearl was growing. She seemed to approach life a little differently than Dylan had at that age, but she was the cutest thing on two legs, my little Pearl. Dylan had always been a cuddly sort of child. He loved to climb into our bed when he was old enough and the three of us would embrace in a bear hug. Pearl was never like that. She seemed to have a little world of her own. But of course, we thought, each child is unique.

It was when she started repetitively tapping the back of her head against the sofa for prolonged periods that we began raising our eyebrows. It was quirky but soon lost its novelty. She was twenty months old. Other kids we knew had odd routines before going to bed, but not like Pearl. Unless we stopped her, she would bang away all day emitting a groaning sound that came from her chest. The more time passed, the more frequent and aggressive the tapping became.

Worry set in. Alicia being the proactive person I've always known her to be, went online. As the kids slept soundly in their shared room, we went through the many different characteristics she had developed: the head tapping, finding objects that formed matching pairs and incessantly tapping them together to the point of insanity, her lack of eye contact, and delay in repeating words. All the signs led towards autism. We sped through an autism questionnaire and ticked yes to nearly all of the twenty questions. The results indicated that life for our little Pearl was not going to be the same as for

Arc

her brother. It felt like a death in our family, plain and simple. We went through all the stages of grief: shock, denial, bargaining, guilt, anger, depression, and hope, but not necessarily in that order. The future you envision for your child is suddenly snatched away and you are confronted with an unexpected existential question: *what do we do now?*

Not having a clue where to start or who to turn to was like drowning. Who would throw us a life line? Alicia found parents who had autistic children in online forums and sought advice and help. I just sat there and sobbed my heart out. In the evenings that followed our realisation, when we got into bed, each of us would take turns in mourning. One would wail and scream and the other would console, then the roles would be reversed. We didn't sleep.

Our plan of action was to take her to the doctor and get a referral for a psychologist who could diagnose her. But the doctor laughed me out of the office and said she was far too young. I told him I knew my kid and that I was not walking out the door without the letter. I think it took two or three visits and a stern telling off on the phone from Alicia before he acquiesced and we got what we were after. The grieving had been replaced with pro-activity. We had no idea if we were going about things right but at least we were moving.

The battle would be long. So many different tests awaited us: hearing tests, brain scans, and MRI's. She had to be naturally asleep for all of them so on the days of the tests I would get up at

The Second Lap

three in the morning and wake her. We would sit on the sofa watching TV and then take a taxi to the hospital in the afternoon. If there was a delay in the appointment, I would have to keep her awake until the medical team was ready. Once she was conked out, they hooked her up to all sorts of machines and ran their tests.

Each visit to the hospital reminded me that we weren't in the most desperate straits. Seeing wards full of kids who could barely drink through a straw or even get out of bed put it in perspective. There was just so much involved before the actual diagnosis came in July 2009.

Getting the official pronouncement was a milestone and a jumping-off point for the next steps that we had yet to figure out. Our daughter was autistic with learning delays. *Why us?* It was pointless to ask, but I still asked it. *Why us?* She had a one in a billion big brother and parents who would lay down everything for her; we would fight.

Our families took it in different ways. Some relatives accepted it and felt great sorrow and sadness. Others were sceptical and unsure if it could even be detected in a kid who was about to turn two. Either way, we didn't have the time nor inclination to worry about how they felt.

Autism is sometimes known as the invisible illness—you can look at an autistic child and not know a thing is wrong with them, unless your eye is trained. Nowadays, I can spot an Asperger's or autistic kid from ten feet away and usually within

Arc

a few seconds. They carry themselves in a certain way and sometimes have what is known as 'stims.' Stimming is a repetitive body movement that self-stimulates one or more senses in a regulated manner. Stimming in professional circles is known as 'stereotypy'—a continuous, purposeless movment—hence, Pearl banging objects together and her head against the sofa.

In a nutshell, autism is a lifelong developmental disability that affects how a person communicates with, and relates to, other people. It also affects how they make sense of the world around them. The earlier the diagnosis, the better. It meant we had a head start. Going to various seminars, meetings, appointments, and talking to parents over the past few years, I have seen how much of an advantage it gave us to have Pearl diagnosed early. It didn't make it easier but certainly gave pause for thought.

After months and months of tests and meetings, we locked in our team of professionals: psychologist, speech therapist, and physical therapist; I then had to make sure she got to them all. People sometimes ask me where I learned French. Was it through courses, TV, DVD's? Nope, I learned French from having to go to three appointments a week with French autism professionals and by conversing with the teachers and administrators at the local crèche. I told the *crèche* folks that she was a little fairy who was different but worth taking a chance on.

It was out of necessity and because I absolutely loved every strand of hair on the heads of both my

The Second Lap

children that I learned how to get by. I got flustered and did plenty of sign language and had a drinking problem, but when it came to those kids I gave them my all and more. I love that unknown quote: "You don't know how strong you are until being strong is the only choice you have."

In reflection, I sometimes think that Pearl being the way she is saved me. There is always the burning question: *Would I change her if I had a magic wish?* It's a hypothetical that haunted me for years and my response, for the longest time was *yes!* At seven years old, the answer I know now, unequivocally, is *no*. I love my son for who he is, for his intelligence, his humour, his kindness, and his sensitivity. Looking at my daughter, I see all the same traits. She is not disabled. As my friend Agnes puts it beautifully; she is differently-abled. I see a child who lives in a dream world and loves me for who I am. She has no pretence, no agenda, and no menace. Life is frustrating for her because of the endless noise and commotion. And you know what? That drives *me* crazy too, so good for her! She may not communicate as directly as others, but she has visual talents that just blow my mind. She sings like a little bird in the rejoice of spring and she loves the outdoors. She has taught me more about compassion, understanding, and patience than I could have learned anywhere else. She also inspired another passion that completely turned my life around.

22

Strength and Beyond

FOR ALL MY disdain of the French and their irksome, subtle cultural tics, I admired many aspects of their lives. There were very few fat people around. No joke. Having lived in Ireland and England, both fast-food, beer-guzzling nations, I saw plenty of people tipping the wrong side of the scales. The French like the outdoors, a lot. Paris' parks and trails were, weather permitting, full each weekend. Kids roller-bladed and cycled, adults jogged, and grandparents played *pétanque*—everybody was getting physical and even though I cycled everywhere with Pearl strapped in a toddler seat on the back of my bike, they still made me feel positively lazy.

Alicia's uncle, JC, could be seen pounding the pavement each weekend and ran ten to twenty km like it was a short jog around the block. How

The Second Lap

do you run twenty km and not fall over and die immediately afterwards? My brain failed to compute that. For years in the past, any time I was in a car and saw a person running down the road, I let out a chuckle—I found it so pointless; I would wind down the window and shout "Looooossers!" Running around and around only to end up back where you started and stinking with sweat? Nooooo thanks. I'll stick to exercising my right arm, the one with the can of beer attached to the end of it. Runners, pfff! Douchebags, more like it.

Then alcohol got me in trouble, *again*. I was at JC's place and we were hammering rum and listening to Led Zeppelin. Out of nowhere, JC tells me I need to go out for a "run" with him, not a long one but just ease into it. I'd love it, he boasted, and, with a mind intoxicated and full of bravado, I agreed to meet him on Sunday morning to give it a shot. I had nothing to stop me really; the stress of life—a daughter with autism—needed an outlet. I could practice my French whilst chatting to JC on our little jog. My attitude at the time was that I had no life anyway. Running, it wasn't my thing, but it was something.

JC pulled up on Sunday morning in his car and explained we were driving to a flat part of the forest to start. Viroflay is in a basin, surrounded by hills on all sides. Flat sounded good. I looked ridiculous with a beaten-up pair of shoes, crusty blue shorts, and a yellow T-shirt, but the forest was beautiful. I was caught by surprise at the twinge of nostalgia I

Strength and Beyond

felt for my grandmother's home in Ireland and the memories of being a boy there, running wild and free.

JC and I weren't alone. All ages and shapes had the same idea it seemed. Some folks were out for a leisurely Sunday stroll or a light jog, then came the speeders, all lean and glistening with sweat as they powered past us. JC told me it was all about finding my rhythm and just enjoying it. The distance or speed did not matter. We started. I was moving forward, which was a direction that felt kind of good. But even that feeling had its limitations. Our goal was twenty-five minutes. Being a smoker and a drinker, I was panting like a St. Bernard in a heat wave. It astonished me how out of form I was! Seventy-year-olds were skipping past me in exuberant conversation as my head lolled, my chin touching my chest like some zombie runner. It was quite a wake-up call.

I had every reason to want and need to be in good physical shape. Drinking and smoking wasn't more fun, it was just easier, and therein lies the problem with many of our attitudes towards life in general. Our drive to make things simpler and easier is both admirable and crippling.

The lengths we go to in order to take a shortcut or lessen the workload is staggering. We want it easy and we want it now. And the culture around us reinforces this natural tendency. It's a quick-fix culture: buying what we are told to buy, watching the movies we are told to watch, and reading the books that everyone else is reading. Why? Because

The Second Lap

it's the easiest path. Many of us don't explore and discover the world; we are afraid of the unknown and stick to the familiar, even when the familiar is mediocre or downright bad. The familiar is safe, even if safe sucks.

The hardest part is taking the leap, which really isn't that hard. But there's an uncertainty in your mind that tells you it is. It's effort. It's that part of your brain that tells you to have a smoke or go and meet the guys for a beer—that's the quick route to satisfaction. That's the voice you need to turn off—the voice I needed to turn off. Inside everyone is a drive to do something they are passionate about, but that voice rarely gets heard because it's drowned out by everyday interferences and short term distractions. Tuning into it is like tuning a radio, if you keep spinning the dial, all you'll get is a racket, but if you know what you're looking for, if you focus on finding the specific channel, you will hear the symphony. It might take time to find the channel that's in sync with your passion, but you have to start turning the dial and seeking the right station.

At the end of the run I was toast. My legs hurt and I was seeing stars. I swore black and blue I'd never do it again. The week that followed, I was walking like a heavily pregnant penguin. My life continued on as normal—in the safe zone: smoking, drinking, daily chores at home, and listening to the racket in my brain.

The Sunday that followed, I was back for more of the same. It was like a washing machine cycle:

Strength and Beyond

run, suffer, swear, walk funny, swear, repeat. I didn't feel fitter the second week—I felt more gullible for coming back for a second helping—but fitter, no. Week three saw a slight improvement. I had gone on the internet and done a bit of research. There was this phenomenon called a runner's high. I decided I'd chase after that. Surely it was cheaper than the forty cent beers I was poisoning myself with.

That third Sunday, we pushed it to thirty-five minutes and I had enough juice in the tank to run the last few hundred metres at a quicker pace than I had expected. JC smiled at my little sprint and told me I was making good headway.

Three days later I bought a cheap pair of running shoes and a pair of shorts. When Alicia came home that evening, I decided to go out by myself. I plodded along at a controlled pace and concentrated on my breathing. This was liberating. I caught glimpses of people through their living-room windows watching television. *You're missing out guys,* I said to myself rather arrogantly. I was a newbie after all and wasn't even sure how long I'd continue to run. That evening was not one of looking at my watch and wondering when I'd be finished, the effort felt natural, dare I say *enjoyable*. I found a winding trail by accident and chose to follow it to wherever and then the magic came. I had run forty minutes without stopping and for a fleeting moment I couldn't feel my legs touch the dry trail beneath me. I was hovering on auto-pilot, all parts of my body working in unison and internally thanking me for freeing it from the

The Second Lap

tyrannical reign of toxic substances, if only for a short while. I was on a high and for once it was guilt-free. I had run for almost an hour and I was proud of myself. I kept the routine like that for a while: a run on Sunday with JC and then a midweek solo run.

But I was still drinking, and getting caught out more, too. Alicia would find beer cans stashed amongst the nappies and baby formula in Pearl's changing bag, or notice that the whiskey bottles in our apartment looked very depleted all of a sudden. I had to get sneakier—and as anyone who has had an alcohol obsession knows, we can be ingenious in our stealth. I topped up the spirits with water and hid cans of beer in the basement. Any time I went down for a cigarette, I'd neck one and come back upstairs.

Meanwhile, Pearl continued her therapies but struggled to sleep. She rocked and groaned until two in the morning and both Alicia's and my nerves were frayed. We snapped at each other time after time until we agreed it was best if I slept in Pearl's room and Dylan slept with his mum. This would give Pearl company and help her settle. The sad thing was that neither of us protested this change in arrangements. We both welcomed it, I think. We didn't have to lie together at night in silence and not talk about what was or wasn't happening between us. The physical attraction seemed to have faded and all we were left with was ourselves. In essence, we didn't face up to it and put it on the back burner to boil over at a later stage.

Strength and Beyond

I began to love going for a run. It was a freedom away from the numb existence I had come to know. But I still needed a drink. I couldn't drink when I was lapping the miles on the road, but I made up for it when I got home. After my shower, I'd be right down to the garden at the back of our apartment to smoke a cigarette and covertly drink my stock. As a compromise, beers during the day went from six to four but the indigestion if I ran in the evening was wretched. Fifteen years previously, it had been cycling and music that collided, now with running and alcohol, two other fault lines in my life had intersected; neither one prepared to accede to the other. I upped my training to the point where I could run an hour without stopping. The quiet confidence it gave me was simply revelatory.

With that confidence, I decided I would run a marathon. How hard could it be? JC cautioned me it was harder than I thought and advised me to compete in a sixteen km race in a few months time called Paris-Versailles and see how I fared. He would run it too and pace me. Sixteen km, I would breeze it, I said to myself.

JC and I ran a reconnaissance of the route. I was fine for the first half an hour. Then we hit the hill that splits the race up: a leg burning beast that seemed to ascend and then ascend some more. He told me that on race day if I stopped to walk it, I would never restart running. On the practice run, I stopped two-thirds of the way up. It was torture. My lungs screamed for more air and my legs were

The Second Lap

drowning in lactic acid, and there was still half the course left to go. I was severely trounced.

In time I learned that my running was a very introspective affair. I didn't feel the need for people around me as much as I had in the past. Alicia went out with her friends from work; I ran. Was I running away from something? Most likely. However, I also felt I was running towards something. I just didn't know what. When the day of Paris-Versailles arrived, I could barely keep my breakfast down, I was petrified. Sixteen thousand runners, most wearing modified bin-bags for insulation on that clear September morning, lined up under the Eiffel Tower. When the gun went off, JC and I got to work. He motivated me and distracted me with conversation. We took it easy for the flat part of the race and right before the big hill, about six km in, we stopped for water. Then the battle started. People talk about hitting the wall in figurative terms. This was close to literal. Halfway-up, people all around us started to walk. Looking into JC's eyes, he told me not to even think about it. We kept a steady tempo and all I focused on was the ground and my breathing. The hill flattened off after a km but turned swiftly to the right and up a long straight of cobbles for the last sting in the tail, a straight, steep, narrow road that almost brought me to a standstill. Five hundred metres never looked so long. I could feel my saturated headband slipping down my forehead, sweat sliding down my temples and cooling my neck. My back hurt and my knees groaned. The downhill section jack-hammered my

Strength and Beyond

quads and took us through Viroflay where friends and family cheered. That gave me a vital shot of adrenaline to push me over the line in a time 1:24. I couldn't negotiate stairs for a few days after, but I was a real runner now, and the marathon was calling.

The Paris marathon is held in April each year and attracts a world-class field. It is a relatively flat, fast route, and the sights you see make for a visually stunning race. After Paris-Versailles, I had six months to prepare. I read a lot of blogs and got tips online on how to fuel and make sure I made it to the finish line. I had no expectations and only two goals: finish it and enjoy it. I could either run myself ragged, achieve a decent time and have the entire race be a blur, or I could cruise and savour my home city.

The marathon is one of the most unique sporting events in the world for several reasons. The one that stands out to me is that you follow in the footsteps, and run in the same race, as the greatest runners in the world. The ground you tread on is the same as the elites have tread on, only they do it in half the time. That doesn't happen in the Tour de France or any other grand sporting race. I lined up nervously thinking, *will I actually make it?* After all it *is* forty-two km. The longest I had gone in training was twenty-five. Having run a decent half-marathon four weeks before, I had some indication of my fitness level.

I couldn't say I was much disciplined in my training. I had continued to drink like I always

The Second Lap

drank, in abundance. I had cut corners in training to serve my drinking and only stopped imbibing three days before the race. So nerves were a factor.

When the gun boomed and sent forty thousand of us on our way, there was no turning back. I paced myself, took my time and really just smiled my way through the first fifteen km. I stopped at each water station to keep on top of my hydration. This wasn't so bad, really. Then thirty km came. My legs were getting tired and my feet ached from the three hours of running. I knew Alicia and the kids would be at the thirty-five km mark. That gave me the courage to continue, and when I saw them they hugged me and told me to run hard, I felt a surge of renewed energy. I kept my head down and pressed on, crossing the finish line in three hours and fifty seven minutes. I was elated. I had finished, and I had taken my time. I was a marathoner.

Marathoners often say that once you've run one, it changes your life. It *is* a monumental achievement that places you among a small percentage of people who actually accomplish this goal. It's not just the marathon; it's also the tremendous amount of discipline it takes to get there. I think you should get a medal for just making it to the starting line.

It didn't change my life, though. I was very proud of completing the Paris marathon, as were my friends and family, but it failed to light a real fire in me. Life went back to normal, *again*. I looked into more races, but during the rest period after the marathon I didn't run for weeks and fell back into my old addictive

Strength and Beyond

habits with ease. Nothing had changed at home. It was the same crap, different day.

A few months after the marathon, though, I had started running again and was training on the Versailles castle grounds as the sun descended into the horizon. I was thinking about Pearl and about our situation at home. I felt powerless. I wasn't working and had no real purpose. Then a flash of inspiration hit me. I would start an organisation to help bring awareness to autism and raise money to benefit Pearl and maybe other autistic kids too. I would call it: 'Running for Pearl'.

I can't remember Alicia's first response. She probably thought I was crazy. But when I fleshed out the idea, she got on board. Crazy or not, no one ever achieved anything by sitting on their butt. The first person I contacted after I discussed it with Alicia was my friend Q back in Ireland. He agreed to set up a website for me. Over the weeks that followed, we exchanged ideas by mail and I drove him crazy with my attention to detail. Slowly the bones of the idea started to take structure. But I still needed an event to draw attention to my new organisation.

Not long after this flurry of activity, JC and I were on a training run when he asked me to help him with a furniture move the following Saturday—anything for a running partner—for the guy who got me into this fantastic athletic endeavour. It was a predictable move. We passed most of the day in and out of a van lugging wardrobes and beds. It was during one of these forays he casually mentioned he needed to up

The Second Lap

his training. Why? He was preparing for a hundred km race. *What?* A hundred km! I asked him if my French was so bad that I had misinterpreted what he had said. *Mais non,* he was going to run a hundred km. In just one day.

I had so many questions to ask him. Did he stop to sit down and eat, or did he take breaks or a nap? He had done one before and was used to this kind of inquisitiveness. A marathon is impressive, but when you tell someone you have run two and a half marathons in one push, they tend to sit up and take notice. I was drawn in like a moth to a flame, a fly to cow-dung, an alcoholic to a kebab shop. The very attributes that make me an addict are the same ones that lit up and told me *dude, you have to try this*.

I was greeted with derision by almost everyone I told about my plan. It's not possible. You'll die. Are you crazy? Why would you do that to yourself? I had surfed the web and found an entire underground culture called ultra-running, men and women who ran fifty miles, a hundred km, a hundred miles; the possible distances seemed endless—this one in twenty-four hours and that one in forty-eight hours. In the online forums, these ultra-marathoners all spoke of the physical demands. But there was another requirement that permeated the online community discussion as even more important: the mental power an ultra-marathon required. Racers spoke of hitting walls and running through them to reach states of mind on the edge of complete exhaustion, where a higher level of almost euphoric bliss

Strength and Beyond

lifted them out of themselves and enabled them to push on when their bodies should have just stopped.

I wasn't interested so much in the distance by itself; my intrigue lay in the journey and the mindset. This would test how tough I really was. It wouldn't require speed, which was just as well as I didn't have any. It would boil down to eight inches: the distance between my ears. Once my mind was made up, there wasn't a thing heaven or earth could do to change it. After some searching, I picked my race. I would do the 100 km de Vendée in Western France. I set about organising it.

Christmas came and went and I trained reasonably hard; I found a system to drink and still train to the best of my ability. I cut down in the afternoons but got wasted in the evenings. I had beer hidden in the room where I slept with Pearl, and I would sit in bed at night drinking and reading until late.

After four months of training, the week of my first ultra-marathon arrived. The race was scheduled for May 15th—the following Saturday. My mum and sister Alison had agreed to take care of the kids so Alicia and I could make the trip together.

We had a really great time on the journey. We laughed a lot and played music in the car, like we were teens on a road trip. Not having Dylan and Pearl with us gave us a chance to just be together and forget the pressures back home. The town was buzzing as we pulled in. Skinny people with weather-beaten faces walked around nibbling on energy bars and sipping from sports bottles. We

The Second Lap

checked into our hotel and looking out the back window, we could see runners and their crews in the car park dialing in last minute plans and selecting gear for the next morning.

I ate a big pile of food that evening and went to bed at ten P.M.; we woke a little before the three A.M. wake-up call we'd agreed on. Alicia was amazing. She dropped me off at the gymnasium some twenty minutes drive away for the large breakfast banquet, and then returned to pack up all our belongings. I'm sure she was sleep deprived and nervous, but she held it all together for both of us.

At five A.M., we took off into the darkness, a mesmerising line of bobbing headlamps accompanied by the sound of hundreds of feet on asphalt. The first two laps went without incident (the course was six laps of sixteen km). Alicia cycled beside me after lap two which was when runners could have an official companion alongside. The occasional pause for fuel was the only time I slowed down. It was on the fifth lap—some 64 km into the race—that my mental battle really started to boil. I hit the wall and found it extraordinarily difficult to keep any sort of rhythm going. I was reduced to a stumbling walk. The sound of my dragging heels told their own story.

Alicia doubled back on the course to find me mumbling and disheartened. I had a rumbling tummy, aching ankles, and spasms that shot down my calf muscles with increasing regularity. Luckily, she had her game face on and told me that if I could not continue it was OK! But, she told me, I would

Strength and Beyond

forever regret it if I quit—that I had come this far and trained so hard. She also told me that I was "Running for Pearl" and walking was not part of the equation.

So with about twenty km to go, I closed my eyes and pictured my kids. I looked at Alicia and told her I would never quit, ever. Once I locked into the groove, she told me I was on the "PP," the Perfect Pace. Then I ran; I ran to the finish line. When I had sixteen km to go, I stuffed oranges down my throat to keep me from falling over. When it started to rain as I was going up a hill, I took off my hat and screamed at the sky "Is this all you got? Come on!" I was so angry for having walked, so desperate to finish and wondering if there was any way at all I could keep up this pace for thirteen more km.

Alicia had her motivational phrases down to a T at this stage and said all the right things, cracking jokes when needed. Her insight into my state of mind saved the day. I would only find out later that with the really slim saddle on the bike, she was suffering too and never said a word. I pushed beyond what I was capable of doing on physical stamina alone. I cannot tell you what it is like when you pass a sign that reads '98 km'. I saw two or three guys in front and I just went for it. Something clicked and I raced past them with ease. Alicia screamed "RUN, BABY" and pedalled as hard as she could towards the line to be there for me when I arrived. I could see the finish flags and the crowds in the distance as she cycled out of sight.

The Second Lap

Turning into the avenue and seeing people rising out of their seats and calling my name blew me away. When I crossed the line, I saw the clock, 12:21:17. Then I saw Alicia and we hugged so very hard, both crying with joy and heavy emotion. We had done it, together. It was such a deep experience we shared that day. In spite of the tensions arising in our marriage, in Alicia I had a partner who had worked hard at her job to allow me the time to pursue this dream. With my completion of the 100 km race, Running for Pearl had arrived. People flooded to the Running for Pearl website with messages of awe, encouragement, and respect. The race was nothing compared to what autistic kids have to endure every day. To paraphrase one of my favourite authors, David Foster Wallace, *the more vapid and trite the cliché, often the more real and sharp the fangs of authentic reality that lie behind it*. The cliché here was that the experience humbled me so much. This *was* life changing.

23

Honour

IT TOOK ME some time to process the experience. I'll admit, I was overcome by it all. But one thing continued to gnaw away at my insides. I had this double life going on. I was draining more cans of beer in secrecy than ever before and stopped at nothing to fill that thirst. I was obsessive, addicted, and getting to a place in my life where turning back, or even turning left or right for that matter, was becoming borderline impossible. Weeks after the greatest run of my life, I started to quickly and deliberately shut myself off from the world. I stopped returning my friends' text messages and I gave little or no news about the children to my family back home in Ireland. If we were asked to go for drinks or dinner at a relative's place, I opted to stay at the apartment. I just could not function without

The Second Lap

drinking. When I cycled my bike with Pearl on the back to all her medical appointments, I was always under the influence.

And I took other risks with her safety. If Alicia went out of town on business, I took myself to the limit by staying up late at night getting buckled. A beer before bed was essential. I'd have to run to the bathroom as soon as I woke in the morning to purge my body and get ready to do it all over again. Being physically sick was also part of the shame at what I was doing to my family. But I could not stop. I had all this love around me, and yet my two little children were subjected to a dad bent over a toilet bowl every single day. I hated myself.

For years I had gotten by with my alcohol abuse, but now the disease had set in. I was like a house with wood rot, its foundations slowly eaten away over the years, finally collapsing in a pile of debris and dust. I would wake after dreams of death and try to piece little bits of information from the previous day together. I'd meet Alicia in the hallway and have a flash-back of being caught pouring whisky into a glass that should have been just coke. I internally insulted myself. *You're worthless, no one would miss you, you'd be better off dead, you loser, kill yourself and get it over with.* Suicide had entered my mind, and to be frank, I was running out of options. In early August 2010, Pearl turned three years old. Alicia's mum decided to have a big barbecue for her at her home in the countryside. She also invited most of the family. Aunts, uncles and cousins with

Honour

their own offspring made the one hundred km trip to the countryside west of the city. It was going to be a magical celebration for the magical girl whom everyone adored.

Both Pearl and Dylan have something wonderful and funny about them and people who meet them feel it. I say it not because they are my own kids but because reactions to them are always filled with positivity and love. It was a Sunday, and it was a scorcher. Parasols were put in the garden along with a paddling pool to keep the children cool. Meat was piled high on the food table waiting to be cooked. When Alicia's family is involved, it means liquor, hard liquor. Not known as a beer-drinking crew, the majority of them like their whisky and I fulfilled my role as the barman. My routine, after years of honing, was simple: be everywhere and no one will catch you. I'd pour a drink for someone and then a shot for myself. I'd go indoors to the kitchen and drink white wine from the bottle whilst getting sausages from the fridge. I was draining whisky bottles by the neck and when people asked where it all went, I'd hold my hands up and say "Hey, I'm a beer drinker, it's you guys who are putting it away." The master of deflection.

As my words slurred in my mouth that afternoon, I knew I was so very messed up. Alicia gave me the look that I had become so used to. She didn't have to say a word, but it was a caustic glance, *stop drinking*. Be everywhere and no one can pin you down was my strategy. Well, I was everywhere but there. Inside

The Second Lap

my head I became hostile and hateful. I wanted to scream and tell them all to go to hell and leave me alone. I had switched from playful drunk to the depressive alcoholic and kept on going. By the end of the day, my eyes were dazed and I could not speak coherently. Pearl was staying with her grandma for the remainder of the week and Alicia, Dylan, and I headed home in the car. I stank of booze and fell in and out of consciousness as Alicia berated me for how I'd behaved. I had let them all down. Especially the kids! When I wasn't dozing off, I was longing for Pearl who'd be away for the week. I pitied Dylan for the excuse of a father he had.

It was on that journey I said to myself, *Do it today, there is nothing in this life for you anymore but hurt and pain; the kids will forget you and get on with life. You will no longer feel the deep shame and powerlessness that has taken away the person you were. Kill yourself. Today!*

I was extremely drunk when that self-directed rant occurred in my mind, but it almost gave me clarity, as if I had found a way out of the torture. Even if suicide was a sin, and I went to hell, it couldn't be any worse than the living hell I was in. The journey home seemingly took forever and the emotional claustrophobia of the car was stifling.

I needed to get on with my plan, but I wasn't sure how I would do it. I decided I would hang myself. I got in the door, put on my running gear and told Alicia and Dylan I was going to the forest to get some exercise and clear my head. I held Dylan

Honour

in the hallway and fought back the tears because I knew that this was the last time I'd ever see him. Who would his dad be in the future? As I held him, I asked God to bring a positive role model into his life after I'd gone, a man who would inspire him to be all that he could be. I love my son more than anything, Pearl too, but I could barely take care of myself, let alone both of them. Alicia, she would be hurt beyond belief but time would heal them all. In years to come I'd be a picture in a frame that hopefully people spoke of fondly.

I walked out the door and went to the basement. There I started to gather the materials to get the job done. I knew there was a rope there from the time I had been trimming the trees during the summer and had used it as a safety harness, the irony was not lost on me that it was now going to cause my death. I pulled the rope off the shelf and wrapped it up neatly. I then rustled around for a beer that I knew I'd hidden somewhere. I found it, downed it. I tucked the rope into the back of my running shorts and left the basement. It wouldn't be long now.

On my way to the forest, I stopped at the shop and bought a six-pack. I was going to go out in celebratory fashion and hopefully not feel it too much when the rope snapped my neck. I was now all set as I hiked up to a dense part of the forest that was concealed by a deep overgrowth of trees and a ditch. It was calm and quiet on that Sunday evening at seven o'clock. When I found my patch, I knew it was the place. There was a little hollow below

The Second Lap

a grand old tree that looked sturdy and I decided to sit on the bank of the hollow for a while before beginning my final preparations. I thought of the life I could have had and I pondered a sober life and how things would have turned out for me. I then prayed and asked God for forgiveness, but He never spoke back. I drank two beers and threw the rope up over a high branch to secure it. I would then be able to climb onto the branch below that and jump from there, which would leave me dangling over the hollow. When the rope was tight and I'd made a decent enough noose, I sat down to finish my drinks. Again my mind thought of all the good times I had seen and how blessed I was that people loved me. I wondered how Trev would go on without me, how it would devastate my parents and brothers and sisters. I ached over Denise and how she had left us and was I about to do the same to everyone who knew me?

I had to do it now, get it over with. I climbed the branch and took the rope in my hands. I put the noose over my head and secured it around my neck, closing my eyes; I prayed to God once more for forgiveness. My heart beat fast and my breathing quickened before a voice said, *No, this is not the way for you.* It jolted me! I opened my eyes, looked at the ground below, imagined a person finding my dangling corpse whilst out walking their dog the next day, pictured my kids with another dad, my beloved family and friends spending the rest of their lives mourning and questioning why this happened. No, no, no, this was not my time; this was like the

Honour

hundred km race. I was in a low patch and I would get out of it and finish the race of life on God's terms, not my own.

I was sober in an instant and shaking violently because of how close I had come to ending my life, *ending my life*. I carefully undid the rope and edged slowly off the branch towards the ground. When I sat back on the bank, I roared crying. I just tore my vocal chords to shreds with raw screaming, bleeding tears. I was hyper-aware of the intensity of what I had just attempted to do. I was a whisker away from being dead and from ruining countless lives in the process. That was not how I wanted my life to end. I had fight in me and would go on until I beat the devils inside. More demons would come in the future, but I would beat them too. The most important thing was the fact that I wanted to live, and I wanted to love.

I knew that facing reality meant I had to face my marriage, only I was afraid to. A part of me desperately wanted things to work out between Alicia and me, but in the back of my mind I knew that it had gone past that. We led separate and very different lives. She was social, I was a recluse. She went to rock concerts, I went running, when I wasn't drinking. Dark nights arrived in the form of winter and my mood darkened with it. I wasn't going to go out and try to kill myself again, but that was for the sake of others, not for me. It was the ultimate limbo. I had loved ones I believed I needed to live for whilst I myself didn't want to live. I felt it was merely a

The Second Lap

life of obligation. Some people I'm sure would have traded lives with me. I had a roof over my head and food on the table. I appeared physically fit but punished my body through reckless self-abuse.

There were many more reasons to drink as well. Trev had gone to Australia for The Captain's wedding. He and some other friends there phoned after they had been drinking and having a whale of a time. "We miss you, you should be here," they said. I didn't say it, but I thought, *Yeah right, I've got no job, no money and going through the worst period of my life; my own marriage is crumbling in front of me, and I tried to hang myself three months ago. I'll be on the next flight out guys.*

At this point Alicia and I were arguing constantly in front of the kids and ready to strangle each other. We needed to talk it out and on the same day as the Captain's wedding in Australia, December 4th, we did.

There wasn't much drama. We asked what the other wanted to do. We both chose to walk away. It had been stretched too far, too much had happened. We both just needed to move on. Could we have gone to therapy and fixed it? I don't know. At least one of us would have needed to want to go, but neither did.

That night we sat and watched TV and laughed. We were relieved and could talk again without the fear of an emotional eruption or a screaming match. She would be heading to Dubai a few days later to work on a big Christmas gathering she was

Honour

organising for her company. It would give us space from each other and time to try and comprehend what we had decided. When she said good-bye, I knew that there was no going back, and that even though we had acknowledged we were separating, it was going to get a lot worse before it got better. I had nowhere to go and we would spend another year under the same roof with me sleeping in Pearl's room. Being separated and living together is the worst experience imaginable, separate shelves in the fridge, fights over minor things like toothpaste, passing each other in the hallway with looks of contempt. We almost throttled each other at times.

As soon as Alicia was on her way to Dubai, I went shopping for beer. Days all felt the same and between spontaneously haemorrhaging tears and listening to songs that reminded me of her, I tried to keep it together for the kids. I didn't tell my family or even Trev because it was Christmas and I felt I needed to deal with it myself first. I got the kids up in the mornings as usual and continued life as I knew it: school, feeding them, and so on.

I made a trip to the local supermarket on the Friday morning after Alicia had gone to Dubai to buy my stock for the next few days. I needed a steady supply. I would drink beer in the shower, in the morning and at night, on the way to the school and the way back. If I was awake, I was going to be sipping a beer.

This was going to be an absolute vulgar display of intoxication. I dropped Dylan at school, went to the

The Second Lap

supermarket and filled a backpack with thirty-two half-litre cans of beer at five minutes past nine and took Pearl to the park. I drank a few there. Once I got the buzz, all my worries faded. It was clear to me now: I was going to be single and have a great life.

Then I walked Pearl and myself back to our apartment and played with her a bit, and then drank some more. Time seemed suspended until school finished and I had to get Dylan. By this stage I was wobbling a little but spoke to neighbours and people from the town as if I was walking on sunshine, a master of disguise. I now had my two kids, all I'd ever need in life. I sucked down more forty cent beer. I could put away two in the space of half an hour with ease. I even had three on the go at the same time, one in the bathroom, one in the kitchen, and one in the living room, so that in every room I entered I'd have a sip within arms' reach. I knew what I was doing with my kids was wrong. I knew it, but I also was confident that I could be in control. When a person who drinks from time to time has a few beers, they get tipsy and are incapable of functioning very well. My body and brain were accustomed to a perpetual buzz, my kids were probably in more danger crossing the street with me if I was sober than under the influence. Sobriety was a world I did not know. Being constantly drunk was how I managed life for many years. In fact, I excelled at it.

After making their supper and showering them, I tucked the kids in and went on to deplete my stock. My mother would be arriving the next night at

Honour

midnight to help me with the nippers for a few days. Another reason to celebrate. I kicked up to a gear that even I did not know existed. I switched from having beers with a smile on my face to violently gulping them down as I prayed for my mind to be erased, or at least to blackout before the pain inside my head caused another breakdown. I paced the apartment sobbing and hitting myself; the room spun so I lay on the sofa, curled up in the foetal position. The dark starry night was above me, falling in on me. Then everything went black.

I have been disoriented in my time but never had the living daylights frightened out of me in such a way as that moment. I was dying. I turned and saw Dylan. His eyes said it all—he was stricken with fear.

The night came back in flashes; I had gotten into bed beside him (at some stage) because I was lonely and hurting. I had to *crawl* to the bathroom a few times to puke my insides up. When there was nothing left in my body, I kept on vomiting. He'd heard this most of the morning, and after I blacked out I came-to at mid-day. There was a plastic bag on the floor and I just weaved limply over it, trying to get out the bile inside me. The room stank. The kids were starving and I didn't even know where to start. The phone was ringing and when Dylan passed it to me, I could see from the caller ID it was Alicia. Nightmare! I couldn't talk. I opened my mouth, but no sound came out. The passage from my stomach to my tongue burned of acid and cheap alcohol.

The Second Lap

That's when Dylan told me he didn't want me to die. I have never forgotten those words or his face at that moment. I knew the second he said it that I was done. There was no false promise, just the voice of God telling me that it was time. When I put my feet on the ground to stumble to the kitchen and make breakfast, I knew how lucky I was. It's rare that a chance like that presents itself in such a powerful way. I called it a miracle then and I still do. That morning and the day after changed the course of my life in ways I never imagined. It transformed my faith and relationship with God and my perspective of myself and the world, it took *me* out of the equation. It showed me that to function as the human being I yearned to be, I had to put others before myself. I had to pay back for all the times I was selfish and self-serving. After twenty years of drinking, I had time to make up for. The first part was getting sober.

When you drink at the level I did, getting sober is the hardest part. One of the biggest reasons alcoholics never make it past the first few days is due to the tremors and other excruciating withdrawal symptoms. How was I going to get through that Saturday, even with my new-found resolve? As soon as I got the kids dressed, I took them to the shop and bought three beers to make it through the day. The first one was drunk on the street in front of everyone to get rid of the shakes. Once the shakes were gone, we went to the park and then to visit

Honour

their great grandma, and I managed not to drink the second beer during that time.

After we got home I downed the second one. I kept the last one for bedtime. When I tucked the kids in, I promised Dylan I was going to stop, that this time I'd prove it.

I couldn't swallow food as my oesophagus was raw from the night before. I drank the last one and sent my mum a text to call me when she arrived. I passed out and woke up again at midnight to let her in. She thought she was seeing a ghost and I said we would talk in the morning. I was so grateful to have her with us that the first thing I did the next day was change her return flight so she could stay a few more days and help me get through it. I never would have made it without her. I love you, mum.

That Sunday we went to Alicia's aunt's house and had lunch. Still very shaky, I barely ate and had a glass of wine with my untouched meal. It was the last drink I ever had. You have no idea the smile on my face as I type those words—*my last drink*. So much of my life up to that point had been devoted to drunkenness. And so much of this book revolves around the subject—you must secretly be relieved, dear reader, to see the back of it.

December 12th, 2010 is as important as my kids' birthdays and more important than my own birthday because I was truly born on that day. It was not an easy birth. The withdrawal symptoms were horrendous. I had to change the bed sheets every day when I woke up. I shook and dreamt of horrors

The Second Lap

no one except those who have also gone through the experience can imagine. It was like a penance and I talked to God every day to give me the courage of my convictions and lead me towards the path of the man He wanted me to be.

When I emerged from that torturous cocoon, I was weak and tired and only found out later from my doctor that I could have died from going cold turkey. Apparently, with the severity of my addiction, I should have been on medicine to lessen the withdrawal symptoms and help my system recover more gradually. I could have had a stroke or a heart attack. I was lucky. No, I was blessed. On the fourth day, I tried a little run but only managed ten minutes before I had to sit on the pavement and walk back home. Baby steps, one day at a time.

My mother left after doing what a great mother does, rescuing her child when he is lost. Alicia returned with stories about her travels. We were all happy to see her and look at her photos from the trip. Our interaction was like that of two friends catching up after a vacation. She asked about my mum's time with us, and I asked her about the cultural differences in Dubai. I did not mention anything about my scare, but she was curious as to why I hadn't picked up the day she called. I fobbed it off with some excuse or another. And life got back to normal; nothing really changed over Christmas as we had already been sleeping apart. Early in the New Year, the Viroflay council contacted us to say they had an apartment for us, and we were glad to

Honour

leave the old apartment behind. Closing the door on that place for the final time was like sealing the casket of a ghost that had haunted me for far too long. Surveying the empty bedroom where I once slept with my beloved wife and had witnessed the miraculous power of God's healing in the form of sobriety, brought me to my knees. When I walked out the front door for the final time, I didn't look back.

I was sober and ready to get back to Running for Pearl. I had been building an online following through the site and social media to spread the word about what I was doing whilst I was boozing, but I never gave it my full attention. Even so, the reaction I got from people I had never even met was incredible. A really global community had come together to support me. Others had climbed mountains, participated in Ironman competitions, and run marathons—every step in the name of Pearl and autism. With new focus, I was determined not to let these people down. There had to be some way of getting back the trust I felt I had lost. I wanted to push the limits beyond convention. In typical *me* fashion I chose a world-record-breaking challenge that had stood for years on my home soil. I would attempt to run Mizen Head to Malin Head.

24

Letting Go

THERE IS A story called 'Footprints in the Sand', the origins of which are unknown. It is a story that has always been dear to me and summed up how the next year and a half of my life would be.

One night a man had a dream. He dreamt he was walking along the beach with the Lord. Across the sky flashed scenes from his life. For each scene, he noticed two sets of footprints in the sand: one belonging to him, and the other to the Lord. When the last scene of his life flashed before him, he looked back at the footprints in the sand. He noticed that many times along the path of his life, there was only one set of footprints. He also noticed that it happened at the very lowest and saddest times in his life. This really bothered him, and he questioned the Lord about it:

Letting Go

"Lord, You said that once I decided to follow You, You'd walk with me all the way. But I have noticed that during the most troublesome times in my life, there is only one set of footprints. I don't understand why when I needed You most, You would leave me."

The Lord replied:

"My son, my precious child, I love you and I would never leave you. During your times of trial and suffering, when you see only one set of footprints, it was then that I carried you."

Mizen to Malin Head is a five hundred ninety km trek from the most southern point in Ireland to its most northern point. It varies by a few km depending on how true a line one takes through the country roads. It has been run and cycled many times over the years and the running record stood at five days and thirteen hours. I was planning to go after it.

In order for me to set a new record, I would have to run a hundred km every day for five days and then tag another ninety km on the last day in less than thirteen hours. On paper it looked doable. In reality, the organising would be beyond anything I'd attempted before. I would have to do the majority of it myself and I launched my newly sober mind into making it happen. I set July fourth as the start date. That gave me six months to make a lot of phone calls and send a lot of emails.

The Second Lap

Training would also have to be done and Alicia supported me which meant I could train the long distances needed to prepare for it. We were still living together, and I won't lie; it was incredibly tense. We fought, screamed, and maintained completely different lives under the same roof. The bigger apartment made it easier to avoid each other, but it also let the tension brew. Yes, the apartment was new, but it was hers, not ours. I think the training kept me out of her hair and she liked it that way. In addition to training, I needed funding and sponsorship. I wrote to Salomon, a trail company that I really liked because of Kilian Jornet, a super-humble and gifted athlete on their roster, and they agreed to give me free gear for the year. I wouldn't have to spend a fortune that I didn't have. I would be burning through shoes.

My running ramped up fast and by February, I would be up and running a marathon at three in the morning and back in time to shower and give the kids their breakfast before taking them to school. Having another run in the evening was not uncommon and running a hundred sixty km a week was the norm. Within weeks, I went from a depressed and drunken mess to a lean and focused athlete. I loved the endorphins rush of pushing my body to its limit on trail runs.

I was also approaching two years smoke-free and felt like I had been gifted a third lung. And my attitude toward life and others changed. I was no longer feeling insular and withdrawn. I reached

Letting Go

out on a training site I used to try to connect with Parisian runners. Cue part one of the 'footprints' story. I came into contact with three guys, Christian the bare-footer, René the playwright, and Tim the stud. They are all very different guys, unique in many ways, and having them as friends is a blessing.

Tim Meier was a guy I connected with immediately. Before I ever met him face to face, we traded jokes and stories online and through text messages. I agreed to come and watch him compete at the half-marathon in Paris just to see what he was like in person. We hugged like long lost friends and I knew that I had found a soul-brother.

His story was fascinating, too. Tim was a twenty-nine-year-old pastor from Ohio who had been in the city for a few years as an assistant pastor at an international church in Paris. He had two boys and an adorable wife named Rachel. And he could haul tail. I had followed his training and was inspired how he came back from injury to running killer races. It was only a matter of time before we were meeting for lunch, and hanging out and talking about music. On hearing I was a drummer, he was keen for me to come and see him at the church where he led a worship team that played for the Sunday services.

As much as running bonded us in the beginning, I must admit that it was something we rarely did together or discussed. There was another dimension to the way we communicated. I spoke openly of growing up in a Catholic environment that did nothing to inspire my faith, about my loss over the

The Second Lap

divorce proceedings Alicia and I had started, and how addiction had almost ruined my life. He listened with patience and grace and encouraged me in little ways that when added together helped complete the puzzle of my life further down the road.

I was trying to move ahead in leaps and bounds. He made sure I only took baby steps. On the day I finally made it to Trinity International Church, I was welcomed by Tim and his friends with incredible warmth. The service was complemented by the beautiful and poignant music his group played. The message resonated with me, and as sceptical as I had been about churches, I didn't feel out of place or constricted. Of course if the folks back home knew about Catholic me sitting in a Protestant church, I would have been lambasted, but it didn't bother me *at all*. My relationship with God had always been private; I felt sometimes I had to put a lid on it in front of others. Or maybe it was that I hadn't discovered the right *vehicle* for expressing it openly. I found sanctuary that day and during the hour and a half I spent there, I actually felt the chaotic world around me had stopped spinning for just a little bit. Tim was heaven sent.

As the training escalated, I decided to enter a competitive race to get some time on my feet. Searching an online racing calendar, I found a trifecta of races all taking place on the same day, the six, twelve, and twenty-four hours of Feucherolles, about half an hour from home. These types of races are as tough as it gets because there is no limit to the

Letting Go

distance, it's just you and the clock. With a hundred km, you can try to speed up for the last ten km and finish the suffering, but when it's a time-based race, you have to run until the time expires. The person with the furthest distance after the elapsed time is deemed the winner. In spite of my drinking, I had run a track race over twenty-four hours, with mixed results, the previous year. I opted for twelve this time. The course was a slightly undulating loop of 1.2 km. All races would begin at ten o'clock on a scorching Saturday morning in May. The objective was simple, run around in circles when you hear the gun go off, stop twelve hours later.

The day of the race, a guy named JP approached me before the start, having seen the Running for Pearl website and was interested in the cause of autism. He was aiming for big things during the course of the day, whereas I was just aiming to log twelve hours on my feet.

The first few hours were nondescript and consisted of regular water and snack intake, sponges of cold water on my neck and face, and making sure I was well covered from the increasingly hot sun. By the time I had passed my first marathon (3:50) the temperature was hovering around 28 degrees C. I kept my salt intake regular, since I was drinking more and more.

JP was definitely in the zone at an early stage looking strong and tactical. Mid-afternoon brought the real test of patience and mettle as seeing the six-hour finishers wrap up a solid day's running

The Second Lap

meant I was still only at the halfway point. That's when my inability to pee regularly became an issue. I felt the need to urinate, but the colour (think iced tea) and quantity (very little) meant I needed to super-hydrate. I did a mental check and pep talk, reminding myself that I was in training mode and that with the right fuel, I would cover the next six hours at probably the same pace. I stopped for some bread, cheese, and cold meats at the seventy km mark (6:55) and walked a lap eating slowly. I then took a high-carb hydration drink from someone at the aid station and slowly drank the lot. Pretty soon after I could feel my body's equilibrium restored and I settled back into my rhythm.

All I needed now was for the sun to go down. Once I had eaten, I distracted myself from the continuous loops by hooking up my iPod. A few hours of pre-programmed tunes helped to pass the time. But soon the gentle slopes in the road seemed a lot more taxing on the legs and my ankles were starting to beg me for an ice bucket. Every two to three laps I made a pit stop and sponged my knees and thighs to keep my temperature low. At eight o'clock when it started to cool down, I took the first of two Advil to prevent more pain and swelling.

I was then told at the aid station that I was in second place. This came as a complete surprise to me as I had chosen not to concentrate on the rankings. What came as no surprise was that JP was ahead by about eight km. We ran side by side for a few laps as the last hour descended upon us. I was happy

Letting Go

for him and running against someone of his ability brought out the best in me. When the loudspeaker boomed that we had two laps to go, I revved up the pace and crossed the line after a tremendously fulfilling run of one hundred nineteen km. Hugs were exchanged amongst all the finishers, and it was announced that both JP and I had crushed the old course record of one hundred nine km! It was a day of surprises and celebrations. Never in my wildest dreams did I imagine that I was capable of such an achievement, second place in a race of top-class athletes. I believed in myself again, my pride was back.

Ireland would be another matter. I would have to repeat the same gruelling distances on consecutive days. I rested in the weeks that followed and made calls to companies to front money, camper-vans, food for the team, fuel, accommodations, and many other little things that cropped up. I also hung out with Tim a lot before I went to Ireland. He prayed hard for me and gave me so much encouragement on the build-up to it.

Before I even realised it, we were on a plane to Dublin. Dylan and Pearl would be spending the week with my parents. I would be chasing a dream and held in my endeavours the hopes of not just myself, but the people who had carried me along this far.

Two weeks before we were planning to roll, Granny became very sick, very suddenly. She died in the hospital surrounded by her family and I never

The Second Lap

made it back to say good-bye. Had she lived just a little longer, I would have been able to hold her close and feel the smoothness of her cheek one last time. I wished that my kids would have gotten to spend just a moment with my hero, the woman who made so many lives brim with joy.

25

Yield

THE FIRST THING that hit me when I got back was the number of pubs. I had never returned to Ireland sober and usually the first stop was a pint of Guinness. I felt slightly uneasy and if not for the fact that I had such a huge project in front of me, I probably would have had a harder time dealing with old ghosts. My Granny's house lay empty and cold. I sat in her old chair and prayed for her. I spoke to her and told her my plans, how great my kids were doing and how much she would be proud of them. I blew a kiss to the sky and promised her I would make it all the way in her honour.

With just four days before rolling south to start the adventure, I had little time to waste. I planned what needed to be done and contacted my crew of Mick and Mark Kilgallon, two brothers from Mayo

The Second Lap

who would drive the camper van and cater to my every whim and on-the-road meltdown. Trev was also due to land in a few days to crew and give me moral support. No one knew me better or could get inside my head like him.

The night before, Mick, Mark, and I drove to Ireland's southern-most point and in a beautiful cottage on the coast, I tried to sleep, but my mind raced and when the alarm went off at five A.M., we rose with the sun and got ready to face the route with excitement. I have never witnessed anything as tranquil and mesmeric in all my life, the morning silence punctuated only by the waves crashing against the jagged coastline, the mist that hung over us only added to the mystique. Mick threw together a quick breakfast consisting of fruit and pancakes with jam. After a quick video message, I took off up the coastal path with Mark beside me on a bike and Mick following in the van with the stereo blasting. I was trying not to get too giddy and to control my pace. My mind rambled with all sorts of possible scenarios up the road, breaking the record, failing to break the record, being sick, or suffering from mental and physical pain. Nothing would ever compare to the pain of the life I had as an addict and that gave me enormous comfort. I was now doing something I was proud of and at the halfway point of the trek I would see Dylan and would show him how much I had changed. This is how I wanted my son to see me, a strong warrior prepared to do anything to enhance his life and my own. Pearl would hopefully

Yield

know someday, too, that she gave me a reason to push myself beyond limits.

Not far in on the first day, we were joined by two girls who had read about the story in a newspaper and decided to get out of bed early on a Sunday to join us. It was fun having company and after thirty km together they departed having given me a major boost. The goal for the day was a hundred km, and at the sixty km point we took time-out for a nap and to catch up with my friend Fletch who came out on the road to do some reconnaissance for us. At the end of the day, we hit a hundred km and I felt fairly good putting my head down for the night. The roads through Co. Cork had been winding and undulating, and I hoped tomorrow would bring flatter terrain.

I had hoped. Day two was a big effort; the camber of the road and the extremely poor surface agitated my ankles and my knees. The boys took incredible care of me, making sure I had dry clothes and a comfortable chair at each stopping point. Mick's legendary fried breakfasts were just the caloric feast needed for the mammoth distances I was covering. But the second day came to an end at eighty km due to very inflamed tendons in my left foot. I could tell that it was pretty severe and prayed hard that a bit of ice, elevation, and rest would maybe allow me to knock out another eighty to a hundred km the next day.

We drove for a bit afterwards to find a good parking location and stopped by a house whose owners kindly agreed to let us use a little lay-by in

The Second Lap

front of their gate. It would give us a bit of peace and quiet. They made us sandwiches and tea and Mick went in to visit with them that night. I was depressed and went to sleep.

Waking up on day three and putting weight on my foot was unbearable, I winced immediately. I was feeling down in the dumps until Mick relayed the story of the folks who had been so kind to us. They told him of the tragic deaths of both their sons in separate accidents, years apart, and how their lives had been torn to pieces. The story had Mark and I completely transfixed, then Mick went on to explain how grateful the couple were to still have each other, that God had been good to them, that they could still have a meal and have a roof over their heads after the terrible economic crash that had hit Ireland hard. As a parting gift, they donated a very generous amount towards our cause and sent us on our way with a blessing.

My whole perspective for the run changed in that moment. I had a sore ankle, so what? *Suck it up and keep going,* I told myself. Compared to their story, I didn't know what pain was. Fired up, we got back on the road. After ten km, I was starting to hobble. The tendon inflammation left me with one ankle twice the size of the other, plus we were in the middle of nowhere. I had run over two hundred km but I was not even halfway yet. Thanks to some strategic phone calls from our camper-van, a physiotherapist came to the road-side and gave me the news I was expecting. "Keep going and you'll rip your Achilles tendon."

Yield

I was distraught. I had let people down. I was less of a man for aiming too high and failing. Word got out on the Internet that I had to abandon and offers of support came in to complete it as a relay, some friends offered to assemble a convoy of motorbikes and take the flag for Pearl to Malin. No, I decided. I had started under my own steam so I would finish under my own steam.

We hatched a plan that I would take Mick's bike and our friends would join us when we got to my home with more bikes. When I arrived at the half-way point that evening in Ferbane, after riding a hundred twenty km, I was astounded. Most of the town had turned out to meet us. Mick and Mark had bikes now too and rode into the town alongside me. People cheered and friends I had not seen in over a decade came to hug and congratulate me. I realised that it was now more than just me; we were Team Pearl. I had a massage and did some radio interviews before eating and going to bed.

The fourth day we attacked with renewed vigour. We would now have six on the road with bikes, Mick, Mark, Trev, my friends Neil, and Tommo (who flew in from Liverpool to join us!) My brother-in-law Paul would drive the van. That day over many laughs, lots of agony, and even a few tears we made it one hundred eighty km to our stop, Ederney, a welcoming and hospitable family named the Maguires took us in for the night.

The last day took us on a majestic ride through the hills of Donegal, and we recounted how much

The Second Lap

had happened in the previous four days, what it had changed in each of our characters and how our various niggles and aches were trophies of battle. Approaching the summit to the finish line, my team paved the way for me to lead them home. Trev stayed on my wheel and reaching the top, my emotions exploded as a thousand thoughts rushed my brain. I had run two hundred km and cycled four hundred five in four days and eight hours. All I really remember is dropping my bike and helmet and burying my head in my hands as my friends crossed the line. We hugged, we laughed (I cried), and we stared out over the sea in disbelief. We all had achieved something special and we had done it for a cause greater than anyone of us as individuals. The money raised would help to continue Pearl's therapies and give her the best possible chance at a decent life.

What had started as a scripted solo adventure had taken on a life of its own and I was all the better for it. The lesson I learned was yet another from the 'footprints' story—when you need to be carried, put your faith in God and, in the form of your friends, He will carry you. Even though the original plan failed, I had refused to give up and made the most of the hand I was dealt. That made me all the more proud of the trek. When life is like that, and threatens your Achilles' tendon, you can let it defeat you, or you can get up and find another way to keep moving forward.

26

When Faith Conquers Fear

Six months later.

DECEMBER 16^{TH,} 2011. Changing lanes, literally and metaphorically. As I pedal I'm thinking of my divorce court hearing three months away. I look over my shoulder, signal, look again. Then it hits me. The cacophony of Parisian traffic is silenced as I fly through the air in slow motion, my bicycle soloing towards the curb. I am in free-fall until my left foot lands in the rear-wheel spokes of the motorbike that has just struck me. I can't move my leg, but there is no panic. I kind of laugh at my luck, or lack of it.

My first thought goes to my Pearl who I'm due to pick up in twenty minutes to take to her physical therapist. I limp towards the pavement having released my foot from the Salomon

The Second Lap

mountain-running shoe it was encased in, while the motorbike rider curses and swears in frustration before he finally releases it and throws it at me. Then he takes off.

That was how I faced into Christmas, with a mangled foot and desperately trying to find a place to live. Friends' sofas had been appreciated, but I needed to find my own home and prepare for life as a single dad. I had started teaching English after returning from Ireland and enjoyed meeting people and helping them make progress in their jobs. With my own life, I still had a ways to go, and the last thing I needed was to be in a hit and run.

Getting up off the side of that road to reclaim my tattered shoe was a hard struggle. How many more knock-downs could I endure? The solace I'd found in running was something that saved me in a spiritual way and the physical benefits I loved too. Now I couldn't even run—fractured metatarsal the doctor concluded. I felt more sorrow for myself than actual anger. Life was moving on for people around me and here I was, mentally and physically beaten down again. I was praying hard to find a new apartment and felt like a piece of string being stretched to its limit. How long before it snapped?

With the help of many faithful friends at Trinity Church, their blessings kept me going. I endured because a part of me knew it was a test. Every cloud has a silver lining I was told repeatedly. I'd had enough silver linings. I just wanted the cloud to go away—the cloud of my divorce from Alicia, for

When Faith Conquers Fear

example. The papers went through on March 6th and it was a sad day for both of us. I wasn't prepared for how empty I felt after, but the healing could really begin now. I eventually found a little nest for me and the kids to share on the alternate weeks I would have them.

I was becoming more forgiving of the acrimony between myself and Alicia. I too had said hurtful things and wanted to heal the part of me that had, at times, lashed out in anger. I worked hard to be a better human being and give back the love I had been shown by so many people. I could feel the old me coming back, but the foot was relentless. Even after the all-clear from a sports specialist, phantom pains seared the ball of my foot first thing every morning. A three-step walk to the bathroom in the middle of the night was a pain-filled limp. I would sit on the edge of my bed at four A.M. and cry, a shaft of street light illuminating my shaking hands. I prayed hard to overcome my despondency, but at times it became too much. Why did it hurt so much mentally? I had known intense physical pain from many endurance runs before, so where was my will to push through it?

I've discovered over time that will is one of the strongest characteristics I have, but it is truly irrelevant without patience and faith. I had to be patient and I had to have faith. I spent my non-running time by going to races and cheering on Tim and Christian and other friends. I filled my prayers with wishes of success for *them* and not for my *own*

The Second Lap

recovery. How, they asked me, was I able to watch so much racing and not participate? Was it not hard for me? It was harder than I realised in the beginning, but seeing how much it meant to *them* erased every shred of wanting to trade places. We are complex beings, but our fundamental role should be to take care of each other and be there through good times and bad for the ones we love, including the ones we may not even *like*.

During this difficult recovery period, I was fortunate that music and worship occupied my life on a deeper level. Being part of a loving group at Trinity Church sure did make life sweeter. I also started this book.

One particular Sunday I happened not to be playing the drums and sat with my friend Tony and his family to savour the message. Our wonderful pastor, Al, introduced a smiling pastor named Ron who would talk a little about healing. I didn't know Ron or anything about him, but he talked about travelling the world and how the power of belief and healing had changed many lives. From terminally ill people to folks with ailments that made life seem insurmountable, he spoke of true miracles that brought an almost tangible energy to the room. "What's this guy been smoking?" I murmured to myself. I believe in God, *love* God, but all this talk of healing and rebirth! Let's just say I was dubious. But I had nothing to lose. I thought of my foot; I held my hand over my heart and wished away all the sadness that I had carried for too long now. As

When Faith Conquers Fear

our worship team played softly in the background, Ron asked if anyone would like to be healed. Seven or eight people stood up, and even though I wanted to, I was reluctant. I felt my legs raise me up and my inner voice tell me just to let it all go, free myself and dump my baggage.

Ron instructed those present to touch the person standing. Tony gripped my left shoulder hard and with purpose. With my eyes closed, I felt another palm touch my right shoulder. I opened them to see a man, a total stranger, filling me with his love—his wife and son holding onto him. As Ron prayed, he asked us to tell our pillars of support how we needed to be healed. I thought of my foot, but I felt to pray just for that would be selfish. Many more people are worse off than a guy with a messed up foot. So I asked to have my heart and soul healed. Tony prayed beautifully for me as did this man who was pouring out every ounce of God-given love inside him. As my emotions grew, I said the silent prayer that I had said so many times. *Please Lord heal my foot, make me the person I was and more. I will honour You with every step if You can get me back on the road.*

There are some experiences in life that just cannot be quantified nor explicated. My breath skipped momentarily and I felt like I was having a sort of panic attack. I could feel the hands placed on my body warm up to an almost uncomfortable level of heat. My chest felt larger and my heart expanded as if it was filling with air. Had I not been in the

The Second Lap

circumstance I was in, I'd have been calling for an ambulance such was the unfamiliarity of this feeling. Tears were cascading down my face, my shirt looking like I had just stepped out of a shower of rain. As the music faded, I opened my eyes. I had been filled with the healing power of the Holy Spirit and was now seeing the world through the eyes of Jesus. His love and mercy pouring out of me. Peoples' faces looked different, life looked different, better, more in focus, not as rushed. I hugged Tony with all my might and then turned to this beautiful family of three who propped me up at a pivotal time in my life. A few seconds later they were gone. Nobody knew who they were, they had never been to the church before and no one has seen them since.

Two days later, I went on another one of my attempted runs expecting a forgone disaster. The previous ones had all ended after two km usually, but this time I ran light and easy for seven km. *Disbelief* is the word that came to mind. I hadn't run that far in the last seven months combined. The next day I did the same and the following week the distances increased and my lungs couldn't even keep up with my foot any more. No more morning pains, bye-bye bathroom hobbles, running meant more to me than ever.

Before, I had been obsessive about my running and could only appreciate long, four-hour slogs. Today even walking up a flight of stairs brings me joy. I am currently running in the way I once did.

When Faith Conquers Fear

Physically, I feel great; however, it's the mental aspect of it that for me has been forever altered.

I took a lot of steps back to make those few vital steps forward. The challenges I've faced have all been footsteps in the greater plan laid out before me. Because of these struggles, I appreciate, beyond words, the good things that come into my life. I can really smell the flowers and take time to teach my kids what matters. I lived the glamorous and quick-fix lifestyle. It sucked; it was a vacuous hole filled with forgettable experiences and empty, materialistic trappings.

I have learned that nothing can fulfil us unless we deepen our faith in the Lord. And having a relationship with God does not mean praying for nice things. Changing jobs or relationships doesn't magically fix our problems, it only puts them off until one day we have to look in the mirror and realise that materialism is not synonymous with happiness. I call it my lottery analogy: I quit buying my regular Friday lottery ticket a few months ago. Why? Simple, because I don't want to win. What would realistically happen with a large sum of money that would make me any happier than I am now? Everything I have fought for would lose its value. I believe in the lessons my Granny Mahon taught me about hard work. I don't want the changes in my life to be cheaply obtained by chance, I want them to be earned with my own sweat. Life can be hard and messy, but as I learn through my mistakes and put

The Second Lap

the pieces together, I find myself growing into the person I want to be.

I have learned to distance myself from condemning voices and surround myself with people who love me for who I am. I love my children, my family, my friends, my God, Running for Pearl, music, writing, raising autism awareness, and many other things. By working hard on each of these areas of my life, I have received bounties that cannot be measured. I am living the life I always wanted but never thought possible.

Jesus truly saved me and there's no turning back.

Having faith, real faith, a faith that will catch you when you are falling, is about giving and loving. It is about opening your heart wide and never losing your belief in the glory of Jesus. Even if you don't believe, just take one step towards accepting Him as your Saviour. You will *not* regret it. It is about trusting Him and bringing His love to others in times of need. Jesus heals all when we surrender our hearts and minds to His power which is all-encompassing and everlasting. Live in the present tense and be the best you can be. Someday it will all be over and what you leave behind can be decided right now, in an instant. It's a decision you make to go the distance. Your footsteps may wander and your legs may become weary at times, but if you choose love over fear, the world will never, ever be the same again.

Epilogue

ON A FORGETTABLE April evening in 2012, I came home from work and slumped on the sofa. As much as I wanted to chill and watch back to back episodes of *Breaking Bad*, I felt called to write. What? I didn't know. His voice just said *Write*. And so I did. It started off as a type of journal, dissecting parts of my life in hopes of laying certain ghosts to rest. *The Second Lap* is what poured out. I didn't ever think that it would become a book, let alone one that mentioned faith or God. But, I began writing anyway. Then, when my friends, Josh and Jenn had me over for dinner one Autumn evening as I was nearing the end of this manuscript, they lent me *Blue Like Jazz* by Donald Miller. In it, I found a writer questioning his faith, religious organisations, and being open about his own fears

The Second Lap

in life. It gave me courage. That's when I knew I wanted to glorify God with the talent He gave me.

As the Lord continued to work more and more on me, I could feel my faith grow stronger and deeper. Such blessings, though, raised questions from people who have known me a long time. Old friends stopped sending the regular messages they used to. Some thought I'd joined a cult or a sect, and I am sure many others have spoken (negatively) about me behind my back. I had always struggled to be myself, but through my relationship with Christ I can be the person I want to be.

Non-believers always say the same things to me: "Yeah, but you can live a good life *without* Christ and *without* a church." Actually, I can't. I have been a believer in Christ my whole life but until a few years ago was not in a relationship with Him. And there is just no comparison between being a regular fixture at church for one hour a week, phoning it in, and being a relentless, devoted follower of Jesus. Going to church doesn't make you better. What it does is give you a community and foundation to pursue Christ *together*. Fellowship is so important. There is no in-between with Jesus either; you can't just sit back and *kind-of* follow Him. It's all in, no-holds-barred devotion.

Yes, it sounds strange. Yes, it's not what 'normal' people say. But what is *normal*? I look around and I see a lot of miserable people—fretting about their jobs, money, relationships, cars, looks, the latest fashion trends, whatever their immediate worry

Epilogue

might be. These things are demoralising, if you let them be. I put my faith in Jesus and walk His path. Life isn't always peachy, but I pray every minute of the day, not just for things, but in thanks. I am at peace with who I am and my past mistakes.

When someone says "Man, you've changed." My reply is, "Of course I've changed." Being reborn sounds cliché, and I know there are crazy televangelists who make decent Christians sound like David Koresh, but I was given a new life, a second lap, and it is my actions, not my preaching, that will define me. I always believed that people who went around saying they were reborn deserved to be in the nut-house. Look at me now. The head should never rule the heart. All of the great music, poetry, scenery, emotions, fears, hopes, loves, and so on that enhance our lives are things we cannot make sense of with our brain. They tug at our *heart*-strings, that inexplicable place deep down inside us. Who looks at a beautiful sunset and tries to break it down to pure, theoretical science? No one. *He* made all of that, and then He made you in *His* image. Beautiful and unique, there is not another like you. Our hearts are the very core of who we are and by refusing to follow them, we short-change ourselves on true and lasting happiness. Surrendering to Christ and praying daily can help us become all that we are supposed to be; a vital part of the grand plan He laid out for us by taking *our* sins and dying on the cross. It is a path of love and wonder.

The Second Lap

Two years on from writing *The Second Lap*, my children continue to grow into their remarkable personalities and I find myself married to a woman beyond compare. When Val came into my life, I knew she was chosen to be at that Thanksgiving dinner in 2012. I wrote her after our first meeting professing my feelings of admiration. She seemed so kind and thoughtful that if I didn't write to her, I would have regretted it forever. She said her heart belonged to Jesus which made me love her more. Over seven months we wrote, as friends, and occasionally hung out when she was on a trip to Paris from the Black Forest in Germany where she lived. God was working in my life and even though I would have given anything to be with Val, the fact that it wasn't happening must have been down to Him. When Val wrote me a nine page letter in July 2013, professing that her heart had shifted more towards a deeper relationship with me, I was floored. The first thing I did was fast for twenty-four hours and pray. I asked the Lord where to go, what to do. And the next morning He told me to meet her in London where I would be shooting some video footage with Josh and Jenn. I have never looked back. Val is a woman of God and has a kindness that overflows in absolutely everything she touches. Every person who meets her is enchanted and she listens with patience and profound understanding. She is beautiful inside and out, and she is mine!

All of these changes in my life have been based on faith. All the dreams I have ever wished for are

Epilogue

coming into fruition because I go to Christ for all my needs. I pray for all who have held this book in their hands and read to the end, that they may take something from it that can move their heart closer to Jesus. And if your heart is already close to His, then pass this book on to someone who doesn't know His love and tell them to read it with their heart. I am thankful and blessed to have been the pen in His hand. God bless.

—Malcolm McLoughlin
Spring 2015

Printed in Great Britain
by Amazon.co.uk, Ltd.,
Marston Gate.